C000127665

BLUE STEEL

THE US NAVY RESERVE

BLUE STEEL

THE US NAVY RESERVE

George Hall and Jon Lopez

OSPREY
AEROSPACE

To all who have served

Published in 1992 by
Osprey Publishing Limited
59 Grosvenor Street London W1X 9DA

© George Hall and Jon Lopez

All rights reserved. Apart from any fair dealing for the purpose of private study, research, criticism or review, as permitted under the Copyright Designs and Patents Act, 1988, no part of this publication may be reproduced, stored in a retrieval system, or transmitted in any form or by any means, electronic, electrical, chemical, mechanical, optical, photocopying, recording or otherwise, without prior written permission. All enquiries should be addressed to the Publisher.

ISBN 1 85532 207 2

Editor Tony Holmes
Page design Paul Kime
Printed in Hong Kong

Front cover Illustrating just how well equipped today's reserve really is, a slick six-ship formation of 'heavy metal' cruises over the Pacific for the benefit of the camera. Only the antisubmarine warfare assets of Carrier Reserve Air Wing Thirty (CVWR-30) are missing from this stack

Back cover Carrying just a Cubic Air Combat Manoeuvring Instrumentation (ACMI) pod on its centreline station, an A-4F 'Super Fox' of VFC-13 'Saints' breaks away from the camera-ship and heads off in search of a Tomcat or a Hornet to 'play' with

Title page Prowling over the Fallon weapons range at height, a pair of F/A-18A Hornets from VFA-303 'Golden Hawks' keep on the lookout for 'enemy' fighters whilst the remaining aircraft of the Air Wing 30 head in to the target on a full Alpha strike mission

Right An E-2C Hawkeye takes off from its shore station trailing a veil of smoke from its two Allison T56 turboprop engines. Once on station the aircraft's three air control officers may be handling five or more intercepts simultaneously, with new bogeys coming on-screen that have to be processed. The aircraft's onboard computers, linked to the radar, will give the airborne targets' course, speed and altitude, and will assign a symbol to the contact for ID. There's a 1500-page manual that explains how it all works. Naval Flight Officer (NFO) training is 28 to 33 weeks long, and the pilots will spend three to five months at the Fleet Replacement Squadron (FRS) learning the aircraft's systems

For a catalogue of all books published by Osprey Aerospace
please write to:

**The Marketing Department, Octopus Illustrated Books,
1st Floor, Michelin House, 81 Fulham Road, London SW3 6RB**

Acknowledgements

We would like to thank the US Navy, Chief Office of Information and Commander Naval Air Reserve Force, New Orleans, Louisiana, for their co-operation and help in arranging visits to several of the fleet's aircraft carriers and naval air stations, and in permitting us access to Reserve Force operations. We are indebted to the following individuals who helped with this project; Rear Admiral Richard K Chambers (Ret), Cdr Dennis Beaver, and Cdr Phil Hazelrig (CAG-30) and his staff. Likewise Cdr Rick Miller (CAG-20) and his group; Cdr Scott Beaton, Cdr Roy Seth, Rosario Rausa, Roy Grossnick, Capt Steve Keith and Cdr Brad Poeltger. A very special thanks to Cdr Mike DiBiello for the exceptional efforts that he made in providing the author with insights into aircraft carrier, air wing and current naval aircraft operations. Thanks too to Tony Holmes for his fine editing, ongoing patience and good humour. We are also indebted to others, who, each in their own way contributed to the book; Anna C Urband, Stuart Leuthner, David C Quinn and Eleanor E L Smith. To each and every reservist who shared their experiences, and in doing so helped to make the book that much better, we are most grateful.

Jon Lopez and George Hall
October 1991

Right Four thirsty F-14s of reserve squadron VF-201 'Hunters' pull up to a KA-3 of VAK-208 'Jockeys' and start tanking. The latter squadron's symbol is, appropriately enough, a whale over a compass rose, this emblem being visible below the aircraft's canopy. The KA-3 also carries the 'AF' tailcode of CVWR-20. A true naval veteran, this aircraft still wears the old Navy paint scheme of grey over glossy white, whilst the F-14s are sporting the monochromatic grey-overall camouflage. 'The Hunters' of Dallas carry the stylized outline of their homestate of Texas on their tails

Contents

F-14 Tomcat

F-14 Tomcat Radar Intercept Officer from VF-202 'Superheats'

'The first thing you notice as you walk around the aeroplane is its size. Gone is the two-tone grey-over-white glossy paint scheme. This reserve aircraft, like those of the fleet, is all non-specular grey. The F-14 is covered in "warning" and "how to" stencils. Before a mission we will begin by conducting the aeroplane's inspection. I'll start on the right side and the pilot will be on the left and we will work clockwise. We will look for loose fasteners, unsecured panels, no FOD (Foreign Object Debris) in front of the jet, check hydraulic reservoirs and look at the pressures, the engine intakes, the brakes, wheels and tyres, the main landing gear and struts, hydraulic lines and electric lines, and in the rear the engine bays and the "tail feathers". I will make sure the variable nozzles aren't cracked and all the lights are on. I'll check the TARPS pod and missile's coolant for the IR (infrared) weapons, the radome on the radar missiles and the nitrogen bottles for pressure to open and close the canopy and to activate the emergency brakes.

'On top of the aeroplane I'll look for any foreign objects in the top of the intakes, loose panels and missing parts. I'll make sure the canopy is unpinned and then check our seats. To prevent actuation of any of the systems the maintenance crews pull most of the circuit breakers while they're working on the aeroplane. I'll reset those, climb in and get strapped to my seat, attach the leg restraints, the Koch fittings to my torso harness and shoulders, connect the G-suit, oxygen mask and then the helmet electrical communications cord for the mike and the headphones. In case of a bailout the leg restraints will pull your legs back against the seat. That will prevent any body parts being left

Right Over the ramp, an F-14 of VF-201 aims for the number three wire. The Tomcat replaced the Phantom II after years of service. One fighter jock recalls, 'Flying around the 'boat, the F-14 is apples and oranges when compared to the F-4. The Phantom II was much more stable at the back end of the ship, and easier to hold on speed and on the glide slope. It had better engine response with its J79s. Once you set and held your attitude you then flew your elevation and the glide slope with power. The F-14 tends to float, and move around, the power being slower to respond. It makes corrections difficult. However, off the front end of the ship the F-14 will fly away without any inputs while the F-4 required full aft stick until the tail became effective as air speed built up. Because the F-14 is not a centreline thrust aircraft – the engines are nine ft apart – if for some reason you snuff an engine while the other is 'cooking in burner' you will have created quite a yawing moment around the aircraft's CG (centre of gravity) which will generally lead to a flat or inverted stall and spin, and recovery from those is slim'

behind in the aircraft when the seat fires. The shoulder parachute harness fittings – SEWARS (Sea Water Activated Release) – are designed to release automatically if we land in fresh or salt water, preventing us from being pulled under by a wind-blown canopy. Our seat and pan houses all manner of goodies: a life raft with a signal beacon; survival radio; ground markers; ground-to-air signal cards; drinking water and 50 ft of nylon cord. There's aspirin, gauze, surgical tape, fresh water purification tablets, insect repellant and a flare gun with shells that burn at 3000 candle power – enough light so that on a clear night the glow can be seen over the horizon by ships at sea. Both the voice radio and the emergency beacon are on the same frequency so one must be turned off or else there will be bleed-over making both useless.

Above A formidable adversary, the F-14 was built around the Hughes AIM-54 Phoenix air-to-air missile and the AWG-9 weapons system, a potent package that enables the aircraft to attack and destroy multiple targets in all-weather conditions, day or night, in its fleet air defence role. This twin-engined, two-place supersonic fighter is capable of attacking six targets with AIM-54 missiles while tracking 18 others

Right The reserve aircraft of VF-201 and -202 form part of mankind's most formidable and complex weapons system – the carrier battle group. The reserve air wing will run exercises and manoeuvres around the clock during the group's 14-day tour aboard the carrier at sea. Seen here are the dedicated Tomcats of the east coast's CVWR-20, aboard the USS *Eisenhower* (CVN-69) in the Atlantic. The 'Hunters' of VF-201 and the 'Superheats' of VF-202 are both based at NAS Dallas, Texas. Their mission is to provide air superiority for strike warfare and fleet defence assets

'Prior to connecting external electric power to the aeroplane I'll turn off the IFF (Identification Friend or Foe), INS (Internal Navigation System), TCS (TV Camera Sight) and the AWG-9 radar. The gyros are caged and the radios are off. Once they connect power I'll check with the pilot on the ICS (Intercomm System) to make sure we can hear one another. When his pre-start check is complete and his switches are set he will "turn the aircraft" to get one engine started and I'll close the canopy. This is done from the backseat because I have a clear view of the entire canopy rail and I can make sure there aren't any obstructions. During this time the ground crew is monitoring for fire and making sure the wings aren't moving. On the carrier, where room is tight, they don't want us motoring out and hitting another aircraft. As the engines come on line I'll listen in on the oral tone stall warnings, the pilot will check the emergency generator and at that point we will start up the weapons system.

'The RIO pushes in the remainder of the circuit breakers. The Computer Signal Data and the Air Data Computers are now on-line. On goes the AWG-9 Weapons System. A check of the coolant light shows "green" and then the INS, IFF, radios and a pull and twist uncage the gyros and bring it all on-line. In the meantime the onboard computer has gone into a sequence of self-checks as I type into the INS the co-ordinates we will be using for the mission – the way-points latitudes and longitudes and our present position – and get an alignment from the SINS (Ships Inertial Navigation System) that's transmitted over Data-Link.

'Once we're on the cat the pilot checks to see that his Stores Jettison Light is out so we don't lose everything when they fire the catapult! Once the checks are complete the pilot comes up on the power and makes sure the Weight Board is correct so the catapult will give you the right "end speed". I'll make sure the pilot gives the controls a good "wipe-out" and that all the surfaces are operating, such as having good forward and aft stick movement and the correct amount of stabilator. The flaps are down with all four lines showing. With a "ready to go" on the ICS, the pilot advances the throttles to burner for the shot. With our heads back against the headrest and going down the track we're looking for a minimum of 100 knots in the next two and a half seconds.

'The airspeed lags so we want to have at least 115 (knots) showing in order to be able to fly. If we don't have that then it's the RIO's job to eject both the aircrew members due to an engine failure or some other emergency. Chances are, even with a single engine on the aircraft at top weight at the launch, we will

Right An F-14 of VF-201 traps aboard the 'IKE' for the start of its two weeks of active duty with the fleet. Naval reserve pilots and aircrews have, on average, six to twelve years of flying experience with the fleet; as a result, this 14-day period serves more as a fine tuning exercise for these seasoned veterans. The purpose of this evolution is to bring all of the air wing's assets together and then plan and execute strikes taking the power projection scenario to whatever lengths the orders demand

Above Two F-14s of VF-202 'Superheats' start to 'dirty up' as they approach the ship, the all important arrestor hook firmly locked in the down position on both jets. The Tomcats are displaying the unit's 'Texas Tail' (red, white and blue with a white star), and they are both carrying the standard at sea external tanks beneath the intakes. On long, straight-in Case 3 approaches the pilots can use the aircraft's ACLS (Automatic Carrier Landing System). Use of this system during Case 2 recoveries is discouraged because of the system's inability to keep up with, and maintain, good 'on-speed' performance when the aircraft turns, banks and is forced to manoeuvre

Right Abeam the 'IKE', a Tomcat of VF-202 begins its letdown to pattern altitude. In air-to-air combat the first thing one notices about the F-14 is its size — it's a large aircraft with a large radar signature, which means it cannot sneak up on anyone. To ameliorate this shortcoming, when the Tomcat is in pure pursuit the pilot can put the aircraft's nose on the target, which limits the F-14's profile and silhouette. On an air intercept mission against an enemy bomber force, the F-14 will perform most of its work at 30,000 ft, a height deemed suitable for a good missile shot. Each fiscal year, the squadron is required to accumulate 3500 flying hours. With only 17 pilots on strength it becomes immediately apparent that this figure cannot be achieved simply by flying one weekend per month. The reality of Naval Reserve Aviation is that these pilots spend almost 90 days per year with the programme in order to fulfil the squadron's flying requirements. This is of course in addition to their 'regular' jobs

get a jet that will fly as long as the pilot doesn't exceed 10 degrees on the pitch attitude or 14 units on the angle of attack.

'Now we're launched let's look at an air combat mission, a fighter sweep. This is probably the most demanding mission we have. Prior to launching, the RIO has a significant number of built-in checks that have to be completed, and a number to be performed after the launch, to ensure that the weapons systems on board and the missiles themselves are operational. The F-14 has a very good built in test system and it takes 10 to 15 minutes to complete a thorough on board check.

'Immediately after we're airborne the first thing I'll do is run through the ACM Confidence Checks on the computer. This checks the missiles on board, the weapons systems and makes sure there is a pulse doppler or a single pulse target track. It checks the Track While Scan System to be sure that we can display up to 20 targets on the TID (Tactical Information Display). It tests the

Right An F-14 of VF-202 fires a AIM-9L Sidewinder missile over the Missile Test Range at NAS Point Mugu. The target is an AQM-74 missile drone (12 in wide by 96 in long), powered by a jet engine. The F-14's M61A1 Vulcan cannon is fixed in its relationship to the ADL (Armament Data Line), but with a radar lock-on the gunsight becomes radar directed, tracking and computing the lead automatically, based on the airspeed, G-strain and other variables

Below You are looking for 100 knots in the next two-and-a-half seconds! The airspeed indicator lags so you will want 115 showing to be able to fly. If you cannot achieve this speed the RIO will eject both crew members. Even at gross weight the F-14 remains flyable as long as 14 units of AOA (Angle of Attack) are not exceeded. Of all the emergencies, loss of an engine off the catapult is the most common

Pulse Search and Pulse Doppler Search Systems and will interrogate other items on the computer that could not be checked on the ground.

'As we approach the operating area we will get a VSL (Vertical Scan Lock) on our wingman and drop behind him and get a Pilot Mode Lock on him as well. We will put the data into the ADL (Armament Data Line) Indicator in the HUD and initiate the system. The weapons system will give an automatic lock-on and keep track of him so that in the heat of combat he won't be processed by the computer as an enemy airborne target.

Above Hoping for an 'OK' pass, this F-14 pilot has sunk a little low and is adding some power. Recoveries are closely scrutinized by experienced landing signals officers (LSOs), each trap being graded and filmed for future reference. Reserve air wings divide their two-week periods of active duty between Strike U at Fallon and time at sea aboard an aircraft carrier. Strike's function is to bring the air wing up to date on current Navy doctrine, enemy threats, recent operational policies and to integrate new equipment. All these aspects and changes are then incorporated into several airborne training scenarios. These evolutions will fall under the broader headings of OAST (Overland Air Superiority Training), FIST (Fleet Integrated Suppression Training) and ATP (Advanced Tactical Phase)

Right The four F-14 fighter squadrons in the reserve are VF-201 'Hunters', VF-202 'Superheats', VF-301 'Devils Disciples' and VF-302 'Fighting Stallions'. All operated the F-8 Crusader and the F-4 Phantom II before receiving the Tomcat. Here, steam from a prior launch clouds the track as the aircraft is directed on to cat one. Note the open spoiler doors behind the wing gloves. Like the GIB ('Guy In Back') in the F-4, the RIO in the F-14 operates the AWG-9 Doppler Radar, and the aircraft's weapons system. Because of its computerized variable sweep wing (20°–68°), the F-14 is amazingly agile and nimble as a fighter, capable of six-G 'bat turn' reversals into an opponent

Above Over the Pacific at sunset, an F-14 of VF-301 flies out to sea to rendezvous with the carrier and start its two-week period of active duty training with CVWR-30

Right 'The difference between a reserve squadron and a regular navy squadron is that a pilot will come into the reserve programme with 1000 to 2000 flying hours under his belt in the F-14. When the fleet gets a "nugget", he may have 350 hours total time, he will never have been involved in tactical problems and he will never have been aboard ship, except in flight school. He's had the basics and now it's up to the fleet to train him. We don't have to train anybody. The air force used to hold service-wide competitions until the reserves and the Air National Guard won them all. When you've got guys with between 2000 and 4000 hours in tactical aircraft, competing against people with 300 hours, who do you think will win?' – Former skipper, reserve fighter squadron

'Once we've established and completed our confidence checks on the weapons and have transitioned into the target area we will assume a combat spread, a mutually defensive position a mile and a half abeam of each other, with some significant altitude spread as well. At this point once we get a vector from the ER-2 that we have bogeys in the area the RIO in the lead aircraft is responsible for running the intercept.

'In an air combat engagement we ideally like a good 40- to 50-mile set-up to give the AWG-9 a chance. With a target the size of a fighter, an F-5 or an A-4 for example, we're not going to "see" him beyond 70 miles. In training situations we are more often constrained by the airspace limitations (imposed by the FAA) than by the weapons' capabilities. In actual combat we would be looking for the enemy at the longest distances possible. Heading in we will be using the Pulse Doppler Search for the first contact, then we will switch to the Track While Scan for the first half of the intercept to get an overall picture. If there is more than one target we will be able to see them on our Tactical Information Display (TID). We will be conducting communications at a specified cadence using pre-briefed terminology with our wingman. We can confirm what we see with our wingman and the E-2, to check if they're holding the same thing on their radar. The E-2 will give us a specified point in space – a "Bulls Eye" – whose co-ordinates we've typed into our computer. The E-2 will say, "we have targets 40 miles north of the 'Bulls Eye' at medium altitude." We will confirm by saying "Fighter One seen" and our wingman will confirm the target or targets as well. Very quickly I'll designate a specific target for each of them to shoot at long range and assume a defensive posture to minimize the opponent's weapons system. Usually the Rules of Engagement will establish the firing latitudes. These are always pre-briefed items that are established by the air group commander. If the rules require that we're close to visual range before we shoot we will be looking first for smoke in the air, or any indication that the bogey has fired at us. We would then be clear to engage.

'At this point the RIO's single purpose is to get the pilot's eyes onto the target for an early "tally-ho". The pilot has a diamond symbol on the HUD that shows him where the target is in space. The radar is locked on and as the target comes into visual range he should see it inside the diamond. Once the pilot calls "tally-ho", we will check our airspeed, altitude, our wingman's position and scan for any other targets, then take our shot at this guy with a radar missile.

Left One of the holes in fleet air defence was closed with the design of the look-down/shoot down system that could be employed against wave-skimming anti-ship missiles. The F-14's chunky (1291 lbs/586.5 kgs) Hughes AWG-9 radar has that capability, while its track-while-scan mode lets it lock-up and shoot at the most threatening targets with its store of AIM-54 long-range, AIM-7 mid-range and AIM-9 short-range missiles. With a take-off weight of 55,000 lbs, the Tomcat is larger than some World War 2 bombers, and has caused some observers to redefine the term 'fighter'

Above One of the rituals practised by aviators the world over is the pre-flight inspection. Although the detailed work is carried out by dedicated maintenance personnel, it is still considered good form to do it yourself. Rather than just 'kick the tyre and light the fire', the crew will perform a thorough walkaround. They will look for loose fasteners and unsecured panels, as well as checking hydraulic reservoir levels. Engine intakes, brakes, wheels, tyres, landing gear and struts, hydraulic and electric lines, the engine bays and the tails' moveable surfaces will all be visually ticked off. Finally, missile coolant for the IR weapons, TARPS pod attachment points, radome, and nitrogen bottles for emergency brake pressure and canopy closure will all be inspected before the crew straps in

Left The F-14 carries a crew of two, and it is a matter of front and back seat co-ordination that gets the job done. On most occasions the RIO is the Mission Commander, being responsible for constructing the mission's parameters, operation of the on board weapons system and performing the debrief. Targets and missiles fired outside visual range are also the RIO's responsibility, targets inside falling to the pilot. Weapons selected will depend on the type of target, its airspeed and altitude. When operating with ships like the AEGIS missile cruisers and E-2 AWACs, the RIO will insure that the information presented by his tactical computer matches that emanating from supporting assets on target threats

'When we start manoeuvring my job becomes more complicated. I'll be looking for hostiles and friendlies. Particularly in training exercises we're interested in avoiding mid-air collisions, in not "busting minimums" and in keeping the pilot updated on what the gauges are saying so he can keep his head out of the cockpit. A running commentary on airspeed, altitude and fuel consumption helps so he can keep his scan outside.

'Data Link can also tell us when it's time to fire the weapons. An E-2 designated symbol will come up on the TID to mark an airborne target. We will do a correlation between our INS and his to be sure we're both looking at the same target, and once this has been confirmed the symbol will brighten on the screen, a pointer will appear on the target, and that will be the one we've been assigned.

'In a fleet air defence scenario, if there is more than one target, the computer will designate automatically the target that is the highest threat in Track While Scan mode, or the target can be designated by the Air-to-Air Warfare Officer from the ship by Data Link, or from the E-2 by Data Link or voice command. The target will be designated on the TID. In the FONO (Firing Order Numeric), targets will be identified by number as one, two or three, the highest threat being FONO One. When we get inside the missile's launch acceptibility parameters for the target an indication will appear on the TID in the form of a box around the target. It's called a LAR (Launch Acceptibility Region) and it gives the range and azimuth that the missile can be fired from. We will "fly" our aircraft into that box and receive a range indicator on the target's velocity vector. It will tell us how fast we're closing on the target and the maximum and minimum range markers for our missile, and where we are in relation to the target. Once inside the optimum range the target symbol will start to flash and the RIO's trigger will light-up. The "hot trigger" is the sign that we can launch the missile. If the RIO doesn't want to accept the firing order from the E-2 he can designate another, or if he thinks his wingman has a better probability for the "kill" then he can pass the designation to him.

'Although the Phoenix can be fired from the front or the back seat of the F-14, using the "in-range" indications on the HUD (Head-Up Display) or those

Left One doesn't strap into these aircraft, so much as put them on. Leg restraints are fastened and will draw your legs back against the seat at the time of ejection; Koch fittings clip you to your seat at the shoulders and hips; the G-suit ('speed-jeans'), oxygen mask and the helmet's electrical leads are plugged in for communications. The SEAWARS (Sea Water Activated Release) fittings that connect you to your parachutes riser lines are designed to let go in fresh and salt water and prevent a wind blown canopy from dragging you underwater. The seat and seat pan also house all manner of goodies including the life raft, food, fishing line and flare gun shells that burn at 3000 candle power. The 'E' on the F-14's flank is a Unit Excellence Award, and it sits ahead of a 'Naval Aviation 75th Anniversary' decal. Note too how all the 'warning' stencils are in subdued shades of grey.

Above A brace of F-14s depart 'Fighter Town USA' (NAS Miramar, California) on a simulated fighter sweep. An ACM sortie is probably the most demanding task issued to the crew. Immediately after they are airborne the RIO will run a series of ACM 'confidence checks' to ensure the condition of the weapons system and the missile's onboard status. The Pulse Search and Pulse Doppler System will also be tweaked to ensure target tracking accuracy, and the Track-While-Seen primed to allow the tactical information display (TID) to cover the maximum number of targets. He will get a Vertical Scan Lock on his wingman so that the computer will not process him as an enemy target once they are in combat. Transitting to the target area in combat spread, the RIO will start to take 'bogey vectors' from the E-2 once the radar checks are out of the way

Right With the 'pre-start' check complete, the groundcrew 'turn the engines' and monitor for any signs of fire. In the meantime, the RIO is firing up the weapons system, the Computer Signal Data and Air Data Computers, and the radios, as well as uncaging the gyros and allowing them to settle down before launch. The aircraft's location — the latitude and longitude stencilled on the parking spot — are entered into the INS, along with the mission's on-route aerial way-points. With a call to 'Clear left and right' from the pilot, you taxy out of the blocks

generated by the computer in the back, the Sidewinder can only be fired from the front. The RIO can designate the target for the missile by getting a radar lock-on and having the pilot cage the missile to where the radar is looking and fire it. We also have a gun and it is fixed in its relationship to the armament data line of the aircraft. We look for a radar lock on the target in this mode so that the pilot's gunsight is radar directed, and it tracks and computes the lead based on the G, the airspeed and other variables, which gives him a very accurate gunsight.

'Our low altitude stuff is for fighter escort and tactical air reconnaissance for intelligence prior to a strike, or for post-strike photos and target assessment. The TARPS (Tactical Air Reconnaissance Pod System) pod carries three cameras; the KS-87 which is a forward looking or vertical camera; the KA-99,

Left A reserve F-14 with an adversary F-5 and A-4 slightly aft and below return from an ACM hop. In today's air combat arena, if you 'see' your target you have made a mistake. Modern radar systems should give the crew a 40- to 50-mile set-up on their opponent, the RIO using the Track-While-Scan to get the big picture, with the targets coming up on the TID. The F-14's Television Camera System (TCS) can be aligned with the radar and used for target ID outside of visual range

which is a "pan" camera with a single frame that extends from horizon to horizon; and the AED-5 infra-red camera which we use for road wrecking or mapping. It will give us a continuous running record of an area and can be run for 20 minues before it runs out of film. The pod is a 2000 lbs addition to the aircraft. It hangs between the engines and is controlled from the back seat. The TARPS mission is a high work load for the RIO. We're not only operating the cameras, we're providing navigation and turn points for the pilot on his HUD as well. I'll use the TV camera so I can spot the target in advance.

'I am an engineer by training and a rancher by profession. On the average I spend 12 days a month with the reserve. The squadron makes a two-week deployment each quarter because of training facilities availability. There is no supersonic training allowed in the DFW (Dallas/Fort Worth) area so we have to go where that tactical training is available, and when it's available. Fallon, Tyndall, Miramar, Key West and Oceana have supersonic training areas.

'We did a human factors engineering study for the Navy a few years ago on simulator sickness and found out that RIOs, on the whole, don't get airsick. To make it through the RIO training programme we have to have a high tolerance to motion sickness, an innate defence. In the training programme they put us in the back of a T-39, close all the windows, remove all the visual clues and manoeuvre the aeroplane around. If you can make it through that you can make it through almost anything.'

F-14 Tomcat Pilot from VF-201 'Hunters'

'In 1986 when the movie *Top Gun* came out it made us all famous, but it didn't change the way we do business. It let the world in on a secret that we've known for a long time — that flying fighters is fun. It's challenging, it's rewarding and it's terribly unforgiving if it's not done correctly, but that's part of the thrill of flying high performance aircraft.

'In the early days one of the restrictions that we placed on pilots transitioning from the F-4 onto the F-14 was that you couldn't fight the aircraft until you had logged 50 hours on type. We have our own tactics and basic manoeuvring syllabus to make everyone familiar with the jet and once you reached the magic 50-hour mark you went into the air combat manoeuvring syllabus and once that was completed you were cleared as a "filled up round" in the aircraft. It doesn't fly like the F-4 as the engines aren't as reliable. There are things you can and cannot do with the aircraft, systems that you have to respect and if you do that you will have no problems. For example, you wouldn't do an outside loop because you would have fuel flow problems to the engines during that period of negative G. Basically, in the air combat arena you're not prohibited from doing anything but you have to respect those TF30 engines!

'The biggest drawback to me with the F-14 is that you're so far back on the power when you're flying the glide slope that corrections become very difficult. It's a low drag aircraft in that configuration. Line-up corrections become harder because your wing span is so large – greater than 60 ft – so that line-up becomes critical. Roll control is initiated by the spoilers so every time I make a line-up correction a spoiler in the wing pops up which necessitates a power correction to maintain the glide slope.

'In air-to-air combat the first thing you notice when you transition to the F-14 is its size. You don't sneak up on anybody. It's a much larger aircraft and we have a big radar signature that is larger than the F-4's. In pure pursuit we put the nose of the jet on the target and that limits our profile, and depending on the background or the sky, whether it's a hazy day or if you're coming in low to high, we will try to maximize our ability to get in undetected.

'If we are on an air intercept mission going against bombers we want to get up to 25,000 to 30,000 ft to get our longest range shot. In air defence, going against an F/A-18 of an F-16, we will go down to where they are. In one-v-one with the F/A-18, that aircraft is the favourite because of its thrust to weight ratio, better pitch authority and better slow speed flight characteristics. The limitations that we have with the F-14 are the engines. They've been de-tuned

Above Sometimes the Rules of Engagement (ROE) demand a visual ID and you cannot fight city hall. Closing to within 20 miles on an enemy aircraft, the RIO's job then becomes one of getting the pilot's eyes onto the target for a 'tally-ho', and the diamond symbol on his HUD will show him where the target is ahead. With a radar lock-on as it comes into visual range, the target will appear inside the diamond. At this point things move fast as the RIO will give a running verbal commentary; heading, altitude, airspeed and fuel state, while checking on the wingman's position and for other 'bad guys'. The E-2 will be providing target range, bearing, airspeed and altitude through Data Link ('Dolly Link') to the F-14's TID, and will also direct the crew to the attack heading for the final intercept if needed

Above In a fleet air defence scenario the targets are designated in one of three ways; by the F-14's onboard computer; by the E-2 through Data Link; or by the Air-to-Air Warfare Officer with the battle group. Information on the target and the on board missiles' launch parameters are on the TID. The pilot will 'fly' the Tomcat into a computer generated box-symbol to meet the missiles' launch parameters. Maximum and minimum range markers will appear on the screen and the enemy target symbol will start to flash when you are within optimum 'kill' range. The Phoenix can be fired in 'launch and leave' mode by the RIO or the pilot using 'in-range' markers on his HUD. Sidewinder shots and the gun are from the front seat only

and de-rated and they suffer from compressor stall problems at high angles of attack.

'In terms of experience our pilots and RIOs are probably the best in the world. All have six to twelve years with the fleet flying fighters. In the past, there was a real hesitancy on the part of the regulars to accept the reserves. The perception, even in some high ranking places, was that the reserves are a big flying club and a great place to go when you get out of the regular Navy. In actuality nothing could be further from the truth. People are under the impression that we are weekend flyers and that's all we do. We operate under a training matrix put out by CNAVRES and, like the fleet squadrons, we have training blocks that we need to check off. Our flight programme is 3500 hours per year for the squadron and it should be immediately apparent that with 17 pilots we can't fly that off working weekends. The average squadron pilot flies right at 150 hours per year. The highest total I've ever seen was 300 hours by a reservist, and you can't do that flying one weekend a month! We fly 48 regular drills annually, plus 72 additional drills and participate in active duty evolutions from 14 to 90 days per year — all that in addition to holding down a regular civilian job. Every one of the pilots assigned to our squadron works for an airline, which takes them away from home between 12 and 16 days per month.

In addition to that they are gone for four or five days a month — on occasion 14 days — with the Navy. It's a big sacrifice on everyone's part to participate in this programme. I love fighter aviation and I love the reserves and you will never hear me say a bad thing about it, but it does not come without sacrifices. I think it's important that people recognize this.

'The squadron always strives to be ready for mobilization, but there is no way that we can increase the frequency of training. All our pilots and RIOs have civilian jobs and most of the companies and corporations that we work for are very lenient and give us the time off that we need to devote to the programme. However, you can only go to your boss so many times and tell him you have to be gone for two or three weeks before it becomes unreasonable.

'There are three priorities that have to be addressed if you're a member of the reserve: your job with the Navy; with your civilian employer; and your family, and not necessarily in that order. I think I am successful. All my life I had aspired to be the CO of a squadron. I never wanted to drive a ship or be an admiral as there is no life after flying fighters in the Navy!'

Above A low-viz Miramar-based F-14 of VF-302 with Sparrow and Sidewinder AAMs. The Tomcat is also capable of air-to-ground attacks. With the target's position safely in the INS, the RIO acts as a safety observer, giving the pilot 'standby, track and pull' commands based on computer generated solutions for the attack. Going into strafe a defended target, the crew would make a high speed, low altitude run over a specified route; 500 knots and 100 ft AGL through co-ordinates tied into the INS using charts and a wrist watch as a back up. Once at the target, the F-14 would do a pop-up-roll-ahead manoeuvre, strafe and be gone, thus allowing the enemy on the ground a minimum amount of tracking time on the Tomcat

Right At low speed the Tomcat performs just like any other straight-winged aircraft, exhibiting good handling characteristics, and making it easy to manoeuvre behind a KA-6D, KA-3 or KC-130. Usually the RIO will talk the pilot into the basket. In terms of maintenance, the F-14's innards are readily accessible through easy-access clamshell doors. This contrasts markedly with the F-4, which hid every internal component under a knuckle-busting panel, secured with 100 metal screw fasteners. Antennae on the aircraft's spine are associated with UHF/TACAN, IFF and Data Link, with ECM aerials being affixed to the top of both vertical stabilizers

Above 'Thumbs up'; the catapult is ready to fire and the RIO is looking back to ensure that the wings are fully extended. No machine made by man is perfect, and the Achilles' heel of the F-14 was the engines and the ECS (Environmental Control System) which, if it failed, could take out most of the aircraft's hydraulic lines. Supersonic tactical training for the reserve squadrons is not readily available at their respective home bases, so trips to Fallon, Tyndall, Key West and Oceana are often on the cards. The ACM and TACTS ranges at these stations are invaluable training grounds for crews to practise missile employment and tactics. Before participating in ACM sorties, the pilot and RIO must complete two weeks of ground school, 10 hours of dual-time instruction and 50 hours in the cockpit

Right Tail-code 'ND' marks this F-14 as a machine of the West Coast's CVWR-30. With its wings rolled back, this Tomcat from VF-302 is positioned on cat one aboard the USS *Ranger* (CV-61). One of the Tomcat's less glamorous roles is that of tactical air reconnaissance, specially configured F-14s gathering intelligence data and pre- and post-strike photos for target assessment. The TARPs pod carries three cameras for this purpose; the KS-87, KA-99 wide-angle and AED-5 for photo mapping. The pod weighs 2000 lbs, and is mounted between the engines in the aft starboard Phoenix missile position

F/A-18 Hornet

F/A-18 Hornet Pilot of VFA-305 'Lobos'

'The last few years have seen the development of defence systems – surface-to-air missiles and air-to-air missiles – that have made the A-7's task all the more difficult. While other technologies have advanced the A-7 has remained largely a product of the sixties. For the reserve the F/A-18 is a quantum leap for us in technology and performance. The two afterburning engines give us far greater capability in the strike phase, and its ability to fight its way into and out of the target area is unmatched.

'The "glass cockpit" in the F/A-18 is easy to get used to. Students who came to the F/A-18 RAG (Replacement Air Group) who had flown aeroplanes equipped with the HUD – the A-6, A-7 and F-14 – have had no trouble adapting to the weapons management system in this jet. Although you are forced to wear "two hats", that of fighter pilot and the other of attack, the heart of the Hornet makes it easier; the HUD, HOTAS (Hands On Throttle And Stick) and radar. Within three or four familiarization hops they became comfortable with the Multi-Function Displays compared to the tapes and dials that some had lived with for years. The HUD and HOTAS allow you to keep your head "out of the cockpit", eliminating the transitional scan problems and lessening the work load. This is particularly welcome when we are operating in foul weather conditions. The control of the radar, missiles and the gun is with the HOTAS. There is virtually no reason to look down. With the HOTAS one becomes a "piccolo player", moving from the air-to-air mode to the air-to-ground mode and back in less time than it takes to read. Missiles are selected and fired off the HOTAS and bombing and bomb ballistics are also achieved through computer generated solutions.

'In the air-to-air arena we have little problem with the F-14 and the F-15 in one-v-one. The F-16 however, is another story. It's excellent aerodynamically and has a good radar, similar to the F/A-18, but it's like a gnat – it's very small – so even in close quarters during ACM manoeuvring you're likely to lose sight of it at some time during the fight! When fighting the A-4, on paper, if you look

Right The sound and the fury of naval aviation is nowhere more apparent than during a dual launch from adjacent catapults. Here, an F/A-18A Hornet from VFA-303 'Golden Hawks' and an F-14A of VF-301 'Devils Disciples' are made ready aboard the *Ranger*. The yellow-shirted crewmembers are responsible for moving aircraft on the carrier's flight deck. The F/A-18, with its horizontal stabilators fully deflected for the launch, is carrying extra fuel tanks on its underwing pylons

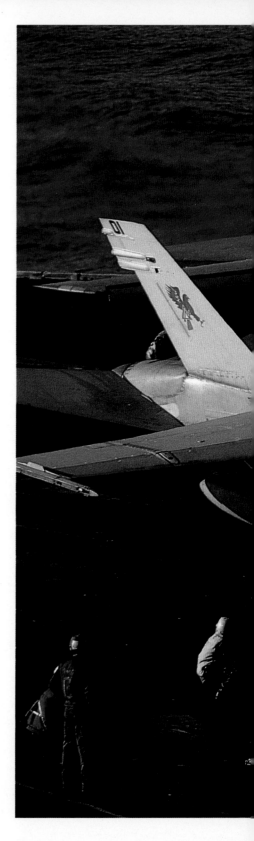

Left The F/A-18, unlike the (A-mode) Tomcat, can take-off on military power alone, its General Electric F404 turbofan engines producing buckets of thrust. The Hornet's flight controls are all computer-enhanced, and when in flight, the aircraft's 'electric' or 'live wing' is constantly moving, searching for aerodynamic perfection under the continually changing variables of altitude, airspeed, air density, temperature and angle of attack

Below Vapour streams from the wingtips of this reserve F/A-18 as it is launched from the carrier. During training, a lot of air-to-air sorties are flown against the reserve fleet Adversaries VFC-12 and -13. On paper the F/A-18 should win every time, but the A-4 jocks know the 'TOPGUN' syllabus inside and out and they are extremely accomplished in the ACM arena. Their 'look-out' is superb, and they can hide themselves in more ways then one could imagine. As 'hot' as the 'Lobos' of VFA-305 are, they will give credit where credit is due

at the two aircrafts' capabilities, the F/A-18 should win 10 out of 10 fights. The reality is a different story. In training squadrons VFA-125 and VFA-106 a lot of air-to-air fighting is done against the fleet adversaries: VFA-127 at Lemoore; VFA-126 at Miramar, VFA-43 at Oceana and VF-45 at Key West. These guys know the TOPGUN syllabus inside out. They are extremely accomplished in the A-4 and in the ACM arena. Their "look out" is superb and they can deploy and hide themselves in more ways than you can imagine. On a two-week air wing training DET they may have 10 or 12 air-to-air engagements per day, so it is no wonder that they are as good as they are. We get our tails waxed by the A-4 more times than we might like to admit. During ACM training one of the scenarios will be to put the adversary up high on a perch and let him roll in for the attack. We must then move quickly to get out of their sights. In another

Above Loaded with Sidewinders and drop tanks, a brace of F/A-18s are readied for launch. They are paricipating in CVWR-30's two-week det at sea aboard *Ranger* as part of the reserve's annual concentrated training period. The wing alternates between time spent at sea, and time spent over the ranges at NAS Fallon, embracing tactics updates and reviewing mission profiles. Once launched, the three primary things that a pilot must monitor to get his aircraft back aboard the carrier are the glide slope, the line-up and the airspeed

Right With one F/A-18 launched, a second moves into position on the catapult. In the air-to-ground attack role, once the target is designated the radar system will search, define and lock-on to it, displaying bomb release information to the pilot on the HUD and the MFD (Multi-functional Display). Extra sensors that can be employed in this mode are the FLIR and the Laser Spot Tracker for fine-tuning the attack. In the air-to-air mode, the radar system uses ranging parameters in the selection and employment of the aircraft's missile battery. Progressing from eighty to five nautical miles, the pilot can use either missiles or his 20 mm Vulcan gun. The APG-65 radar also has RAM (Raid Assessment Mode) for target selection, displaying up to 10 adversaries, and the choice of weapons available, on one of the three CRTs within the cockpit and also on the HUD

Swift, agile and deadly, the F/A-18
Hornet is on the cutting edge of aviation
technology, these two VFA-303
machines seen heading out over the
Pacific Missile Test Range at Point
Mugu. This squadron started life in 1946
flying the F6F-5 Hellcat, progressing on
to the F4U-4, A-4B and A-7A/B over the
ensuing decades. For the reserve forces
the F/A-18 provides a quantum leap in
technology and performance. The two
afterburning engines give the pilot far
greater capability in the strike phase, and
its ability to fight its way into *and* out of
the target area is unmatched by any of its
predecessors

Above Over the Sierra Nevada desert two F/A-18 Hornets from VFA-303, carrying Sidewinders, centreline tanks and TACTs pods, slide into the camera ship's six o'clock position. While stationed at NAS Fallon for their two-week summer training period, the unit will practice close air support target marking and air-to-ground communications as part of the larger FAC programme. The station's Bravo-19 Range is used for bombing, the Hornet pilots aiming their ordnance at old M-47 tanks that have been stripped of their engines, radios and anything else that might be of use, before being turned into 'bulls' eyes'. Video cameras on the desert floor mark the hits from bombs and guns, ordnance delivery signals in turn being sent to Strike's computers for scoring

Left Much to the chagrin of the regular Navy's active duty squadrons (many of whom were still equipped with the venerable A-7E Corsair II), the F/A-18 Hornet made its operational debut with VFA-303, 'Golden Hawks' in 1984. The primary factors in the aircraft's multi-role success as both a fighter and an attack aircraft are the HUD, HOTAS and MFD, linked to the Hughes APG-65 radar. Pilots new to these 'glass cockpits' are often slow to grasp and maximize the system's potential, but quickly come to appreciate it over the traditional cockpit groupings of round dials and tapes. The system has three master avionic modes; air-to-air (A/A), air-to-ground (A/G) and navigation

Above With AIM-9L Sidewinders on the wingtip rails an F/A-18 Hornet from VFA-303 pulls up for a look-see. The Hornet is powered by two F404 turbofan engines, each producing 16,000 lbs of thrust, a force almost equivalent to the aircraft's weight when empty. Up front, the Hornet's 20 mm gun carries 570 rounds, whilst externally the aircraft's nine weapons stations are rated for a maximum load of 17,000 lbs (7711 kg), although payloads of 9000 lbs are more often the norm

Left A Hornet of VFA-204 'River Rattlers', carrying long range tanks, prepares for an early morning launch. Students who come to the F/A-18 RAG/FRS (VFA-125 in the west and VFA-106 back east), and who have flown aircraft with a HUD like the A-7 and F-14, have little trouble adapting to the weapons management system in this aircraft. Although forced to wear two hats the pilot is well equipped to cope with the extra workload. The Hornet's HUD and HOTAS make life just that little bit easier, keeping the pilot's head up and out of the cockpit and allowing him to make weapons, navigation and communications decisions with buttons on the throttle and stick

scenario we will start "neutral" two or three miles apart and then turn and try for a quick missile shot. The way you fight is often dictated by the other guy's first move. If the match becomes a turning fight you can go "single circle" head-to-head or fly in opposing circles, counter clock-wise, only exchanging shots at each other as you pass.

'The F/A-18's flight controls are all computer enhanced. In flight the aircraft's "electric" or "live wing" is constantly moving. You never have to trim the aircraft in the air because of this feature. The computers that are moving the flight control surfaces are continually trying to find the best aerodynamics for the wing at that altitude, airspeed, angle of attack, air density and temperature. The wing is constantly trimming itself under the computers guidance.

'The three items that must be monitored to get the F/A-18 aboard the carrier are glide slope, the line-up and airspeed. Together, they are your angle of attack and the attitude of your aircraft as it approaches the ship. Two of these items are a function of the power that your engine is producing. The F-8 took a long time to spool up while the A-7 was only slightly better. The F/A-18 has an excellent response time from the throttle quadrant. You can end up digging yourself a pretty big hole behind the ship and still have enough power to get yourself out.

'As one of the LSOs (Landing Signal Officers) for the reserve air wing there are some points that I like the pilots to keep in mind. On the approach it is easier to work off a "high ball", being above the glide slope, than getting too low. If you're low there will be two corrections that will have to be made; the addition of power to get back up on the slope, then pulling the power to prevent going through it. Both corrections must be measured in their application and are hard to make particularly at night and in bad weather. Another is that it's better to be a little slow than too fast. It's hard as hell to kill-off that excess speed. You learn to trust the LSO to keep you off the ramp and to get you aboard if you're having a problem. A real bond forms from that reliance.'

Above Wearing a muted grey paint scheme, a reserve F/A-18 prepares for the catapult to fire. Behind the Hornet is a reserve E-2C, which is still marked up in the old grey over glossy white colours. Once airborne, the pilot will move from one mode to another, switching from air-to-air to air-to-ground through manipulating the HOTAS. This proven electronic marvel has removed the navy's need for two mission specific aircraft, and the associated maintenance and parts inventory nightmares that went with them

Right Carrying blue 25 lb practice bombs and a centreline tank, a reserve F/A-18 prepares to take the active runway prior to departure. In practice, as in combat, the Hornets get to their target by flying to a pre-programmed set of checkpoints that have been entered into the aircraft's INS computer. Onroute, steering cues are placed on the HUD with 'fly-to' markers to assist the pilot. At the IP (initial point), and prior to the bomb run, the pilot will receive final targeting information from the FAC; then at 400 kts, dashing below the ridgeline over sand and sagebrush, he will finally pull the Hornet's nose straight up into the pure vertical, roll the ship on its back, pull down into the target and, following computer generated release cues, let the bombs go

A-7E Corsair

A-7E Corsair II Pilot of VA-204 'River Rattlers'

'The A-7 replaced the A-4, with the resulting loss of a positive thrust-to-weight ratio and overall manoeuvrability. The things gained were the weapons systems, the ability to carry more ordnance and the ability to put the bombs where you wanted them to go. Until the F/A-18 came along there wasn't a better bomber in the world. When the A-7 was in its prime in the mid-70s there wasn't another aircraft around that could compare with its avionics, especially when it came to dropping a bomb on target, flying at low-level and getting to the target on time. Some of the navigational and weapons systems in the aircraft are landmark designs. For example, the A-7 was the first aircraft to have a HUD. Over the years the Navy has found components and reworked fittings to improve the aircraft. New radars and new ECM gear was also retrofitted into the reserve aircraft. The A-7 has also had the turbine and compressor blades beefed up to solve a particular problem area. In the late 70s and the early 80s they were losing 12 to 14 jets a year due to engine problems. The engines would stall. Dead-stick landings are prohibited in this aircraft so if the ejection seat didn't work you were in trouble. They've improved the avionics and have tried to keep those in step with the new technologies. The basic airframe, the controls and engine are all pretty stock and have remained unchanged. The controls are all hydraulic, artificial and power assisted.

'You can do a lot of flying in a jet without using the rudders because you don't have prop wash. They are centreline thrust aircraft. Rudder pedals increase the manoeuvrability and the performance of the aircraft especially at lower airspeeds. At high angles of attack it's best to use only the rudder. At slow airspeeds whatever marginal lift you have will be destroyed if you throw an aileron up on that wing. When the aircraft departs it goes over the top. When you go through the RAG (the Fleet Replacement Squadron) they will

Left Two A-7Es from VA-204 'River Rattlers' form-up on a reserve P-3 Orion from VP-94 'Crawfishers'. One of the Orion's roles is maritime surveillance, detecting vessels violating the coastal waters of the USA. Working with the A-7, the P-3 will execute choke-point tactics; the A-7s will lay aerial mines across harbour entrances, thereby denying a belligerent nation tactical access to any strategic location chosen by the Navy. Aboard the Corsair II, the ASN-91 computer provides navigation and weapons release cues through integration of data from the ASN-90 INS, ASN-190 doppler, APQ-126 radar and other nav and comm aides. Information from all this equipment is presented to the pilot through both the HUD and a projected map display

give you a High Angle of Attack and Departure Syllabus where you will do some accelerated stalls and departure stalls, where at full power you will pull hard on the aircraft and it will buffet and then snap over the top. You will not spin it but you will allow it to stall and depart. As soon as you let the stick go it will recover. We will practise anywhere at ceilings of 20,000 to 25,000 ft because NATOPS calls for ejection if you're out of control at 10,000 ft. That's standard for any of the jets. It takes 4000 to 5000 ft to recover and there is some lag in the altimeter as you're coming down. When you get slow the nose tends to wander on you and that's how you can tell that your airspeed is down without looking at the airspeed indicator. The nose starts to slide when you get slow. We've got the Automatic Manoeuvring Flaps now on the A-7 and at a certain airspeed and angle of attack they will deploy; the leading-edge flaps will droop and the trailing-edge flaps will come down to 18°. With these featues it's a much better aircraft; it handles better and now when it stalls it falls straight ahead.

'The A-4 is a basic turbojet and it has good response, so when you move the power something happens right away. In the A-7 we are flying a high bypass engine, a turbofan, so when you add power it takes a while for it to respond. That's the biggest challenge with this aircraft, especially around the carrier. You have very slow power response, the slowest response of any aircraft in the inventory right now, and you have to be ahead of the aircraft with your power corrections when you're coming aboard the ship. The A-7 is a more comfortable, roomy aircraft to fly in than the A-4. With the A-4 when you pull the power back to 80° the spoilers on the wings deploy and kill any lift and that will keep you on the ground. The A-4 is more stable on the runway than the A-7. With its high lift wing and fairly poor brakes the A-7 can be a real handful on a wet runway or carrier deck. The response time of the engine is a trade-off for better fuel economy. The A-7 has probably flown a greater variety of missions than any other aircraft in the Navy. If on the other hand a more sophisticated threat exists – similar to that found in the Middle East – where up-to-date SAM systems are employed and more modern and sophisticated aircraft are used, then the element of surprise would be even more essential to cut down on their reaction time and our losses. In that case, the ship would stand further out to sea, everyone would launch in-sequence and a low altitude rendezvous would follow in order to avoid detection.'

Right Hooks down and in the pattern at 250 knots, the VA-204 pairing of CVWR-20 prepare to recover aboard the 'JFK'. A classic 'mud mover', the Corsair II was developed by LTV in the mid-1960s to replace the ageing A-4 Skyhawk. At the time of its introduction, the A-7 represented state-of-the-art technology, with its advanced flight systems for all-weather operations and autopilot. In its light attack role, the reserve training matrix for its pilots includes War-at-Sea strikes, mine seeding, carrier qualification, air-to-air tanking, radar and low-level navigation, ACM, missile launching with AIM-9s, anti-ship strikes, armed reconnaissance, combat SAR and other bombing and nuclear weapons profiles

Commanding Officer of VA-204 'River Rattlers'

'Normally a strike group would consist of between 20 to 35 aircraft, but if the element of surprise is one of the keys to the operation's success there will be times when a smaller strike force will be prescribed. It takes a long time to get 35 aircraft together. You might want to use a mini-strike of four attack, four fighters to cover them on their way in and one ECM ship for jamming. In this case we would all launch and do a running rendezvous and let the E-2 get us together with vectors on the way in.

'We also have limitations imposed – Rules of Engagement – that are passed down to us from "on high". This lists what targets are off-limits and the "first-to-fire" guidelines. These are subject to change anytime an air wing is going to be executing an operation. The ROE comes from Washington and is set as policy by the CAG.

'There is an order that the brief follows and some of the information is SOP, things we've all seen and heard before. You know from experience what's important and what isn't. You will get a communications plan and the meteorologist will give you the weather at the target and back at the ship. The target weather is important because it will limit or mandate what your weapons delivery is going to be. After the air wing strike brief it's back to the ready rooms where each squadron will review exactly what their element or their division will be responsible for on the strike. It's here that all the small details are ironed out regarding formations. In the A-7 we normally use a combat spread with aircraft flying abeam of each other. This formation is called a "loose deuce". The aircraft fly a mile apart and can manoeuvre freely to cover each other's tail positions. The A-7 is very fuel efficient and we will keep the speed up to 500 knots. With a fuel flow of 5000 lbs per hour we will have about two hours flying time.

'The process of selecting the appropriate weapon is pretty straight forward these days. "Weaponeering" simply requires a manual. It's a "cookbook" with a list of targets, and the weapons you would need to take them out are called out alongside. The bomb's fuse is mechanical and electric. The propeller that arms the bomb is held stationary by a wire that's attached to the aircraft; when the bomb is released the wire stays with the jet whilst the bomb falls free and the propeller is allowed to start spinning. You can see how many seconds of arming time you have by the number of turns of wire. The reason for those arming delays is so the aircraft can distance itself from the target before the bombs go off. In a high dive manoeuvre when you're releasing from 5000 ft at 45° (angle of dive) we like a six to eight second arming delay. Fragments from the Mk 83 can go up to 2500 ft and out a mile or more so you want to be well away from the area. The high dive release at 5000 ft will keep everyone out of the drag area and clear of the bomb blast. The electrical fuse is just an internal electrical element that arms the weapon. There is a control panel inside the cockpit that allows electrical fusing and you can select contact detonation or short or long delay.

'Over our skivvies we wear an olive-drab flight suit that's made of fire retardant nomex. It's light weight and comfortably loose. Next, nylon chaps, the G-suit, form-fitting leggings for your waist, thighs and calves and a parachute harness/survival vest that zips up the front. Over-the-ankle steel-toed boots will prevent us leaving our toes on the bottom edge of the instrument panel should we have to eject, and the leg garters (supposed to pull your leg back into the seat) don't work. And last, nomex gloves with soft leather palms, crash helmet and oxygen mask complete the equipment check list.

'Normally, you would pre-flight the aircraft 45 minutes to launch. The main reason to man the A-7 early is to do an INS alignment, which takes a good 12, sometimes 15, minutes. The more time you give the computer to settle down the better your bomb delivery will be since the ABS (Automatic Bombing System) takes its information from the INS and uses it to compute the parameters for the weapons delivery.

'The pre-flight inspection of the jet varies from one pilot to the next. Some guys just "kick the tyre and light the fire" but I prefer to be thorough. The plane captain (the man responsible for the aircraft's mechanical health) "dives the duct". In order to check for damaged compressor blades and to make sure there aren't any tools left about that can FOD the engine, he crawls down the jet's intake with a flash light and makes a quick visual inspection in the bowels of the beast. In the meantime I'll be checking the skin of the aircraft for loose panels, rivets, plumbing leaks, hydraulic leaks and the tyres to make sure that there's no chord showing. For better speed we will carry the bombs on the six wing pylons, three on each side. Grab them and give them a shake to make sure that they're on securely. The bombs are on two large hooks and are held in place by the sway braces. It's important that the bombs don't roll off those hooks when the aircraft starts to move. Moving aft along the fuselage I check the trailing edge of the wing, the underside of the aircraft and the tail area. I make sure the tail hook isn't cracked and then repeat the same thing on the other side. The wheel wells are a nightmare of hydraulic plumbing and pipes so I take my time there. Usually, the ordnance people will have pre-flighted your AIM-9 missiles and I'll check the nitrogen for the missiles IR cooling. By this time you will be getting electrical power to the aircraft. The "huffer" will be attached to start your engine and it's time to climb in. After I get strapped in the first thing I do is turn the INS platform on, put it in "Ground Align" and turn on the aeroplane's internal computer. If we were at a naval air station we would type in the latitude and longitude that was stencilled on the ground at our parking spot, but since we're aboard ship the jet is plugged directly into the Ship's Inertial Navigation System (SINS) and the vessel's course, speed and position are fed right into the aircraft. The aircraft's INS will keep track of where you are no matter what.

'With the "huffer" connected and Fuel Master "On", the plane captain gives you the "crank" sign. You bring the throttle inboard; that energizes the circuit, and the engine starts to turn. Once you are at the correct per cent you push the throttle outboard; that hits the ignitors and as the throttle goes forward fuel starts to flow to the engine and you've got ignition. At this point the engine takes over on its own. At 42°C the jet's inernal generator comes on line and you've got electricity.

'Once the aircraft is started I'll go through the plane captain checks, move all the controls and check for free-play, plus lower and raise the tail hook and put out the Emergency Power Pack. With the INS alignment complete the "yellow shirts" will "break the plane down" by removing all the tie-down chains that have been securing the aircraft to the deck. Now that I am ready to taxy I'll come out of "Ground Align" on the INS and put it into "Inertial" as I start moving.

'I am looking for 10° nose up on the ADI (Attitude Direction Indicator) as we go off the catapult. Because your airspeed will lag and it isn't initially accurate you will use your attitude reference. So go off 10° and that will definitely get the aircraft climbing. Raise the gear and the flaps and depart out ahead of the ship at 300 knots to the rendezvous point. Altitudes vary and every squadron will have their own. We were the first off today because we're fuel efficient. The fighters will be last and will go to a higher altitude because they will use less fuel up there after they "tank". With the entire strike group together the E-2 will check everyone off for IFF before we proceed over the beach. On a co-ordinated strike like this the E-2 will monitor the airspace and provide you with any "bogey dope" – enemy aircraft movements or activities. As we head inland the *Iron Hand* aircraft – the F/A-18s armed with HARM and SHRIKE – have broken off from the main strike group and have accelerated ahead to points surrounding the target for SAM suppression. With fighters out ahead and in-trail we will ingress at 150 ft in combat spread.

'As we go into the target we will have the AIM-9 stations selected as well as the gun just in case any enemy fighters jump the flight. The weapons select switches are right underneath the glareshield so I hit "Gun-Lo, Master Arm" and stations "4" and "5". The A-7 has no lead computing gunsight. The gun is fixed to fire at a preselected spot in front of the aircraft. This limits its use in air-

Right An A-7E of VA-204 banks back towards New Orleans and home base. Originally designed to carry 1960s' avionics, the Corsair II's doppler, muti-mode radar, navigation and weapons aiming computers, TACAN and attitude reference systems have all received updates over the ensuing years. The Vietnam experience taught pilots that going back to work-over a target twice was a bad idea, and that any urges to do so should be stifled. Many pilots were lost on these second passes. In combat, small-arms fire can be vicious and dense, and when there is the threat of Triple A, target doctrine calls for everyone to stay above 5000 ft

Left Into the vertical, a pair of VA-204 A-7Es climbs towards the heavens, their pilots proving that anything the *Blue Angels* can do the reserves can do even better

to-air combat. It's been suggested that "Terrain Masking" is the best technique for this aircraft to use in an ACM engagement!

'As we approach the target on a low-level ingress, timing is critical due to the free-fall weapons we are carrying. We will have to climb to a higher altitude for their release and that will put us in the SAM envelope. We will have to start our pop-up manoeuvre to achieve weapons release altitude and that's when we become fair game for the SAMs. About the time we start the climb is when we would want the anti-radiation missiles to be on their way to the SAM sites. As we begin our climb the fighters will start their flow around the target.

'One wise-ass A-7 jock once noted: "My primary responsibility is to bring the aircraft back! The second is to get it back minus the ordnance." Well, the A-7 is notoriously underpowered but we've got a lot of airspeed built up on the run in and I'll start my climb to 10,000 ft about 10 miles out. We're trading airspeed for altitude now and as I go up I am running through the Combat Checklist and setting up the ECM equipment. If you wanted flares and chaff to come off the aircraft as you roll in you will have pre-set that in the on board computer before the launch. I select the bomb stations on the master panel and "Normal Attack" on the computer terminal. This puts it into attack mode and places the attack symbology on the HUD.

'As I approach the target I am now at 10,000 ft and off-set by 35°. I pull the nose up, roll the aircraft over onto its back, sight the target overhead and roll back upright, wings level. Now I am in a 45° dive coming down on the target. The diamond symbol on the HUD represents my aircraft and as I rolled in I put that symbol on the target, designating it to the INS with a button on the stick. Now flying by computer-generated steering cues, the aircraft tracks forward over the ground, the aiming symbol walks right into the target and the bombs start to come off the aircraft automatically through a computer generated release. At 6000 ft I'll ease the stick back into my lap and come off the target in a hard bank to the right, looking back to try and catch a glimpse of the damage. Small-arms fire can be vicious and very dense and you would never want to go below 3500 ft in an aerial attack. If there is Triple A with 37 mm you will want to stay above 5000 ft.

'With a quick glance back I'll start jinking ouf of there on the prescribed egress heading using the hills and ridges for cover. Your wingman never wants to come off the target in trail behind you because if they are shooting at you he will fly right into it. You want the enemy to track to different targets. As he comes off the target he wants to get to the inside of your turn so that he will have an easier time catching up.

'As you egress you will be flying a pre-selected ground track and your wingman will manoeuvre back into that combat spread for mutual support. Pre-planning will have assured you that this egress heading will not carry you over any towns, population centres, roads, Triple A or SAM sites. You will more than likely be behind a ridge or a mountain and will be putting some real estate between you and the bad guys.

'As you egress you can start to de-select your bomb stations. Once you're outside the target area and Triple A isn't a problem any more you will go back down to 10,000 ft above the ground with as much speed as you can get and go back out on your ground track. Hopefully, the fighters will have picked you up. Sometimes they will just clear the egress route and will fly independently rather than shepherd you back to the ship. Outside the threat area I will climb to conserve fuel.

'There is generally very little, if any, radio chatter. When I left the ship I would call "Land Launch" and then go to the strike frequency. Coming back you will check in with "strike" once you were "feet wet" or "safe". You will also check in with the E-2 who will have some "return-to-force" procedures for members of the strike force to follow. These could be turns-about-a-point or an area to cross to ensure that no-one is following you back to the ship. You will give the E-2 your fuel state and let them know if you have suffered any battle

Right Looking much like the lush, green fields of South-east Asia below its wings, a VA-204 A-7E overflies Louisiana, its low-visibility grey paint scheme proving totally ineffective against such terrain. Armed with a 20 mm M61A1 cannon, the Corsair II can also carry a broad array of weapons from its underwing pylons including Maverick, HARM, Harpoon, Shrike, Walleye, Wasp and triple Snakeye, GBU-10 and -15LGBs and AIM-9 Sidewinders. A FLIR pod mounted under the right wing can provide data for the HUD, greatly increasing the aircraft's night attack capability and bombing accuracy. An effective tool when used in RESCAP missions, two A-7s will fly a 'wagon wheel' around the SAR helicopter, keeping any enemy threat at bay with its Vulcan cannon until the recovery has been made

damage and tell them where you are. Then you will press on back to the ship, pass over it at the prescribed altitude and go to the rendezvous "stack". I'll talk to "strike" and to the Marshall frequency. They are like Approach Control and then I'll go to the Tower frequency. I'll monitor the Tower holding a certain altitude in the stack until it's time for the recovery and then they will start to bring guys in from the bottom of the stack. You just go with the flow.

'It's about an hour and a half from launch to recovery. When it's my turn to come into the break at the ship I'll come in at 300 to 500 knots depending on how hard I want to make it on myself. At 500 knots if you break right at the bow you've got a lot of work to do to get the aircraft set up because you have to bleed off all that airspeed and try to get set up for the approach. Abeam the ship I put the speed brakes out, slow to 220 and put the gear and flaps out. As soon as you lower the gear and the speed brake a giant 14 ft panel drops out of the bottom of the aircraft. It really slows you down. A mile to a mile and a quarter abeam the ship I start my approach turn, the ship on my left. I'll be about 600 ft above the water at this point, 400 ft up coming through 90° and then rolling wings level behind the boat at 300 ft.

'I use the HUD to make a level turn all the way around the pattern. I put the Flight Path Marker right on the zero pitch line and use the Angle of Attack Indicator. I roll the wings level and put the nose, and the Flight Path Marker, down three degrees — that is the glide path I need to fly to get aboard the ship. Then I will scan the ball to make sure it's centred, check the line-up and check the airspeed. The speed is going to be about 125–130 knots on the way down. On touchdown I'll go to full power until I feel the wire is caught and if it's a good "trap" then it's back off the power as the deck crew start pulling the wire back. As you raise your hook the wire will fall out. I engage the nose wheel steering with a button on the stick and follow the taxy director to a parking space. In the strike de-brief that follows the interrogators are looking for estimates of bomb damage and are eager to learn what the enemy's Triple A and SAM threat were. The brief takes about 10 minutes. As an aid to this the on-board computer has a "Fly-To", "Destination" or "Mark" function. If you fly over something and you want to tell the intelligence people where it is all you have to do is to hit the "Mark" button — a thumb wheel on the stick — and the location will be placed in the computer with the exact latitude and longitude available for recall.'

A-6E Intruder

A-6E Intruder Bombadier/Navigator of VA-304 'Firebirds'

'The aircraft's basic mission is all-weather medium attack at low-level. The jet carries virtually all of the weapons in the Navy inventory. The basic responsibility of the B/N in the A-6 is to act as a bombadier/navigator and a co-pilot. I work the INS system and use radar navigation as a back-up. The radar is particularly useful at night and at low-level because we want to make sure that we don't run into anything. Terrain avoidance and terrain clearance are the official names for that exercise. The bombing portion of the mission at the target can be run off the radar or off the FLIR (Forward Looking Infra-Red) System. It's like a black and white TV screen and it's attached to a laser for ranging to determine the distance to the target and to designate targets to the laser-guided weapons. I back up the pilot through communications work, radios and by monitoring the basic flight instruments in emergencies.

'To go somewhere the INS is first "fed" the aircraft's present co-ordinates, the correct latitude and longitude, and allowed to align itself. Then "waypoints" are entered as checkpoints along the route. Once we are in the air the system is similar to a video game where you put one box inside the other and follow the "fly to" commands. You tell the computer where you want to go and the computer will give you symbols to get you there. If the aeroplane isn't on auto pilot then you've got to fly the A-6 in order to get there. There's a lot of cross checking with charts to ensure that you're where you should be. If the INS starts to drift you can "torque it" – give it manual updates so that it will match your location.

Left An awesome A-6E aboard the *Eisenhower* at dusk. The aircraft's five stores locations can carry a bewildering array of air-to-ground weapons including Maverick, Harpoon, Snakeye, Rockeye and Skipper systems, as well as good old Mk 82s and 84s. Protruding from the Intruder's nose is its characteristic 'Rhinohorn' refuelling probe. To avoid radar and visual detection, the Intruder was designed to fly all-weather, low-level attack profiles. Flying just above the ground below the ridgelines, and using terrain masking to hide its presence until the final moments of the attack, the A-6 crew rely heavily on precise timing, and co-ordination with all the elements of the strike package, to ensure mission success. Fighter elements sweeping ahead to draw off any enemy opposition, *Iron Hand* aircraft armed with Shrike and HARM, and Prowlers turning the enemy's radar and missile defences into electronic interference just as the Intruders arrive to do their work, all combine to aid the bombers' ingress and egress

'Low to the ground the radar system is limited in distance. If your radar picture can see three or four miles and you're going at 420 knots you will cover that distance in about 24 seconds. When the distances between the legs of the flight are 80 or 90 miles at speed you have to keep a running plot in your head of where you are, where you're going and where you've been. We don't just fly over flat and level ground. At night in bad weather, flying through valleys and up and down mountain ridges, you will get St Elmo's fire off the canopy; little tiny sparkles and radio static so that you can't hear anyone, you won't be able to see outside and you will be bouncing around the cockpit like a ball on a tennis court. There are big mountains out there and those clouds can become very solid very quickly, so it pays to stay up with the navigation track and to know where you are.

'In bomb delivery if you need an "angle" on the weapon you're using, if you've got to visually acquire the target before you drop it, then you might use the "pop-up-roll-ahead" manoeuvre. You pull the nose up, roll over on your back, sight the target, roll back upright and with wings level and nose down let the things go. There are also straight-and-level drops — those aren't too dramatic — lofting and over-the shoulder which is another form of the loft delivery but you reverse direction at the top of the loop. The type of target that you're attacking, the weapons that you've selected and the egress route will all be used to determine the mode of bomb release. The terrain will play a part as well. The planning for a mission will have these points covered in the pre-plan study. If the target area is 10 miles long and you're travelling at 500 knots you will be over the target for a maximum of a minute or two and people will probably be shooting at you so you don't want to get there unprepared, without a plan and without a clue as to what to do. What you want to do is avoid visual and radar detection. You will do that by staying low, letting the terrain mask your position from the enemy.'

Left Few other aircraft have seen as much combat as the burly A-6 Intruder. From the jungles of Vietnam to the Persian Gulf, from Beirut to the Gulf of Sidra, the A-6 has worked along war's cutting edge and has given force to Grumman's addage of 'make it strong, make it simple'. Seen at the moment of launch, this A-6E is equipped with TRAM turret, with FLIR and laser in the chin. Basic flight information comes up on the Kaiser AVA-1 CRT, not a HUD but a Head Down Display (HDD) that gives the crew aircraft attitude, nav information and weapons delivery cues. This A-6's leading edge slats are deployed for the launch

A-6E Intruder Pilot and Commanding Officer of VA-304 'Firebirds'

'A lot of the work-up for the A-6 would be similar to that used by an A-7, even for a single aircraft night mission, and that's how we employ the A-6. While you would still have the air wing brief and the fighters and tankers, these would not stay with the A-6 at night. We use the night and low-level ingress as the element of surprise. But the bad guys still have the capability to shoot us down in the dark so we will launch a fighter sweep to go in ahead of us to draw off any enemy fighters that are lurking out there, and *Iron Hand* aircraft with SHRIKE and HARM to work on any SAM sites. In a night scenario timing is critical and everyone must know where they are to be and when they are to be there for this thing to work. All this has to be co-ordinated. Ideally, you would want the *Iron Hand's* SAM suppression missiles coming down on those sites as you go into the SAM's envelope. The EA-6Bs would be there doing their jamming as we go into those envelopes as well. I would be looking for as much coverage from those guys as I could get! All this will disrupt the enemy to the extent that he will hopefully not know the strike is coming, and if he does he won't be able to react.

'On a night mission in the A-6 I would use Mk 82 500 lb bombs. I would have 26 of them on the aircraft and they would be set up for Snakeye delivery – high drag at low altitude. This would be your weapon of choice for barracks, communications shacks, fuel storage tanks, and basically any enemy fortifications that are standing above ground that you want to blow away. In this configuration, the Mk 82 will fall away from the aircraft and large fins will pop open slowing it down. At 500 knots this will allow you to get out of the frag area by the time the bombs go off. On a barracks complex I would drop a pair of Snakeyes every 100 ft. With 20 bombs you would lay out a string 1000 ft long. These are automatically released by the onboard computer.

'For the night strike we might only use two or four A-6s, but this is the key; we are all going to have different targets! No two people will be going in on the same target. It will be a stream raid, head to tail. You're not going to have four jets coming in at low-level in the dark over the same spot because people are going to run into each other. One crew will take the north end of the target, one crew the south. That will provide good separation. We will also mix ordnance so we won't have to worry about running through anyone's frag. Some will carry Rockeye cluster bombs. They are a great anti-personnel, anti-material weapon. They put a lot of holes in things and somebody could deliver a Rockeye five seconds ahead of you and you could fly right over it without a problem, although it does make a hell of a flash. All this is part and parcel of Target Area Tactics and it will let you know where everyone, and their ordnance, is going to be.

'I'll sit down with my B/N and go over the route in a very detailed manner prior to launch. We will talk about ridge lines, altitudes, calls, where we want to be and what we will be saying. By doing this we preclude any nasty surprises or if we don't, when they do appear, we know how to handle them and how to fit them into the matrix that we've mentally established. The B/N uses his radar to keep you clear of terrain. On your side you've got a TV screen, the VDI for night terrain following terrain avoidance. The TV image is based on what the B/N is looking at within 12 to 18 miles ahead of the aircraft. The system takes all the radar returns, selects points from that, puts them in a grid and the computer then gives you a synthetic picture of what's in front of the jet. As long as you "fly" the Impact Bar over the Coded Range Bin you will avoid hitting the ground. This TV picture, your B/N and the radar altimeter will let you see in the dark. The check points and "fly to" steering cues and symbols will also be on the screen and any variations in heading due to cross winds will automatically be factored into and corrected for by the aeroplane's computer.

'The pre-flight of the aircraft and the "walk around" is a ritual. What you are looking for are leaks, missing panels, flat tyres; basically the obvious. The item most likely to fail would be something buried inside the aircraft, something that you can't see. The main wing spar is crucial since it carries the weight of the whole aeroplane on it. Should this be weak and rupture it would happen at a point 10 inches inside the airframe. At a high G load the wing would fail. Only the intrusive eye of the machinist's Magna-flux would discover that flaw but it's not practical to conduct an inspection like that before every flight. So this inspection is a ritual, more form than function. We will check the ordnance too and make sure the bombs have two arming wires, one on the fuse and the other to the fins. Then you will get in the aircraft and do the pre-start checks. With the fuel boost pumps ticking and the "huffer" cranking the engine bring the throttle forward, "around the horn" to hit the igniters and at a certain per cent the engine will start. With both engines running, the B/N will be getting the INS and the computer warmed up and you will transfer power from external to the internal generators. The air-conditioner's primary role is to keep the computers comfortable, not the pilot and B/N, so with that turned up I'll complete the taxy-take-off checks. "Flaperons-Off" is a key item on that list. Used to kill lift, you use those when you want to stop the aircraft on the runway. On the carrier during the launch you don't ever want those things to deploy!

'When you're ready to go you will signal the Cat Officer by turning on your aircraft's lights. When he sees that he will fire you. At night you fly attitude. You're looking for increase in airspeed and an increase in the VSI (Vertical Speed Indicator). Without stores on a single engine the aircraft is flyable but you have to be quick. After checking in at the prearranged rendezvous point the strike group's aircraft will head for the target to carry out their pre-briefed assignments. On the overland portion of the flight we would be doing 360 to 450 knots. As I approached the target area I would get the aircraft moving as fast as I could; 500 knots if it could do it.

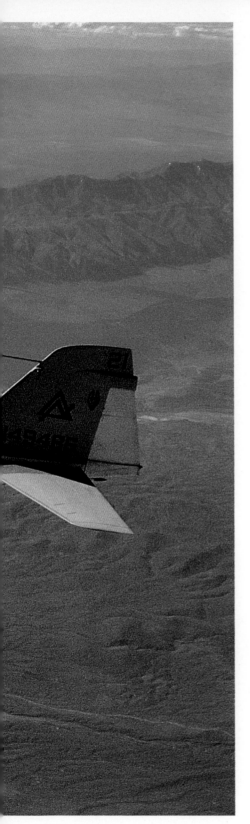

'As you approach the target area the B/N is looking for the IP, and the target itself. These points are in the computer INS and he follows the jet's progress on radar. Target charts and intelligence photos make the site's location on radar easier. Passing over the IP the B/N steps the computer into "Attack" mode and you will start to get attack symbology on your screen. Up until now you were getting steering cues to the way-points; now you're getting them to the target. On your attack display is a white box. Put the box in the centre of the screen, and when you're all centred up and all the other lines stop moving, and your in-range of the target, squeeze the trigger. The sight symbol will slide across the screen over the target and a computer generated release of the bombs will be initiated. The B/N has turned on the FLIR and the laser and now he can see the target on his infra-red scope. This is where the bombs' delivery is fine-tuned. The laser is used to designate a specific building as the aiming point; the range to it is giving constant updates to the computer so as you pass over this "Release Point" all the weapons will come off the aircraft and go through the target. If one used laser-guided bombs, with laser sensitive heads, the target would be illuminated and the weapons will guide on that signal. As the bombs are kicked away the lightened aircraft surges forward. Now it's time to get behind some terrain and head out on the egress heading and get back to the ship.'

Left 'Blue 4', a KA-6D of reserve squadron VA-304 'Firebirds', cruises along at 30,000 ft, high above the desert and salt flats over NAS Fallon. Newly tasked with providing the aerial inflight refuelling duties for CVWR-30, the KA-6 has replaced the KA-3 'Whale' in that role. Internally, the KA-6 carries four 200 gallon fuel cells and mounts a hose reel in the rear fuselage, whilst externally it can carry up to four tanks. During refuelling lights on the basket and the refuelling probe provide the pilot with datum markers for the line-up, approach and hook up, which usually takes about eight minutes to complete. The KA-6 can also operate as a day bomber and as an air/sea rescue controller

EA-6B Prowler

EA-6B Prowler Electronic Countermeasures Officer of VAQ-309 'Axemen'

'We are more than just operators, we are tacticians. We have to have a thorough knowledge of Soviet strategy, on how they employ their surface-to-air missile systems, to do our best work. It's more than knowing what the signal is and when to jam it. The "B" has automated signal processing equipment for tactical updates. There are many elements and many radars that the modern Soviet integrated air defence system will use. If you take away their early warning acquisition radars it makes it very difficult for them to find out where we are. He will also be unable to pass information off to the missile firing complex.'

EA-6B Prowler Pilot of VAQ-309 'Axemen'

'The Prowler handles differently from the Intruder – it's heavier and not as forgiving as the A-6. The "B" is faster and heavier and the approach speed is higher because we have the same A-6 wing but it is stressed with more weight. We haven't had the wing fatigue problems either. We've been lugging ECM pods not bombs and maybe that's the reason. The back seat positions are exact duplications of each other and you don't have to fly with two people back there to complete the mission. Often one person can handle the job because the computers are so efficient. The ECMO's generally alternate front to back. The right front seater assumes the responsibility of the co-pilot and performs check lists, handles the radios and communications chores, emergencies, IFF, navigation on the INS, and runs the HARM control panel.

'We are on a game plan that we are briefed about before we get into the aircraft. We are not threat-reactive. We would be doing pre-emptive jamming based on good intelligence and we would have assigned jamming frequencies ahead of time, if not physically, certainly in planning.

'The two-week period at sea is, in many ways, very productive for the reserves. We will be able to accomplish many of our annual requirements while aboard the carrier including air-to-air tanking, formation flying, ECM, DECM and a lot of other work with the entire air wing as part of the evolution. We don't have the luxury of spending three or four months on "work-ups" practising for the deployment. If there is a war we have to be literally ready to go to sea in 30 days to fight so this gives us the opportunity to work together as an air wing. During the first few days at sea there will be unit level training,

Right An EA-6B Prowler of West Coast reserve squadron VAQ-309 'Axemen' is positioned on the catapult shuttle prior to launch from the *Ranger*. Tail code 'ND' signifies its allegiance to CVWR-30. Aside from the external fuel tanks, this aircraft is also carrying three jamming pods, these high-tech devices being powered by Garrett windmill turbo-generators. Once activated, the pods emit high power jamming transmissions on preset frequencies. The large fairing on the Prowler's tail houses passive signal receivers, part of the ALQ-99 jamming system. Two Electronic Counter Measures Officers (ECMOs) in the rear cockpit monitor this system, the third in the right front seat assists the pilot with radio communications and navigation chores. In the event of an emergency Martin-Baker GRU.7 ejection seats can be employed by the crew

each squadron practising their particular speciality, whether that is fighters, attack or ECM. They will practise in small groups of aircraft. The second week we will be working together in co-ordinated air wing strikes. Because of the level of experience out here the only way you will be able to tell that this is a reserve air wing is by the tail code on the aircraft. Everyone here is an old hand.

'We would have gone through a brief and would have determined where we fit in that strike, where our rendezvous is, emergency procedures, timing problems, mission abort procedures after launch and, depending on the weather, we will have certain attenuating procedures regarding aircraft departures, arrivals at the rendezvous and at the ship, and altitudes for join-up. Case I is good weather, VFR (Visual Flying Rules); Case II is VFR on top, whilst the ship is under the clouds; and Case III is poor weather and one where we will form up and check in on the radio, unless of course we are NORDO or NINCOM and then we will try to use hand signals.

'We will get a rendezvous with a "push time" (a prescribed time to leave) and different elements will break out at different times depending on their targets and what they are going against. Code words will be used to break off the different elements of the strike package. Then at our specified time we will be in a pattern, over a specified spot looking for enemy radars and then at a specified

time we will start jamming. However, based on circumstances you may have to change your plans. You may not be able to do your jamming or lay a chaff corridor because your air cover have been jumped by enemy fighters for example. Or maybe they got lost. Flexibility is paramount. Fortunately, most contingencies have been thought out ahead of time and are in writing. These are the TAC-Notes.

'The mission is all run on a timing pattern but with enemy aircraft out there it's a real crap shoot. We have to keep our heads up. If we go in with a strike group we will want to be at their altitude or slightly above. Our beam is like light from a torch; where the beam is there is protection, so we want to place the strike group in that beam. That's where the jamming is and where they are covered. Our antennas are highly directional and produce a very narrow beam. Atmospheric conditions will also determine where the aircraft are placed. During certain seasons extended ranging of signals at certain altitudes and in certain frequencies bands has been noted. With propagation the signals can bounce off the atmosphere and carry two or three times further. Listening, jamming or being seen by enemy radar will be affected by this phenomena.

'During war-at-sea the "B" will be used due to its electronic listening capabilities and we will be on a surface search by sectors that are designated by the E-2. They will work their section of the "pie" for enemy emmissions and we will also use our surface search radar to prosecute targets. Marine fog layers, cloud strata and temperature differentials in the atmosphere's sub-refractive layers can distort radar returns. This phenomena has altered tactics on many fronts. These conditions can also be used to the attackers advantage. Thunder storms can also generate "target" signals not unlike hard objects on the surface of the ocean. It's not unheard of that a "B" will be vectored right into a storm by the E-2. Anytime you approach a ship you do so with the Rules of Engagement and Deportment in mind and always be predictable in your manoeuvres. Approach from the stern of the ship at five miles and no lower than 150 ft at 230 knots and outside their 500 ft "bubble". I'll dip, take a look and some pictures. I'll never cross his bow, but will turn away. If you pass more than twice it's considered, internationally, an act of aggression. You don't know how the ship's captain will interpret your moves and he may shoot at you or flash a laser at your aircraft trying to burn out the aircrews' retinas.

'Flying Surface Surveillance Co-ordination missions with on board receivers, we will pick up a signal, intercept the origin of that signal, identify the class of

Left An EA-6B with leading edge slats deployed is launched from the *Ranger* as part of CVWR-30's annual two-week tour at sea. This is in addition to CQs carried out several times a year by the squadrons' individually, and not as part of a full wing evolution

ship and radio the information back to the carrier, who maintains a Surface Plot. In training we can stand-off and jam our own ships and they will respond as though they were countering a Soviet force. We will also train against fighters in anti-air-warfare, jamming the F-14's radar. While at sea we will fly perhaps 10 sorties per day with different tasking for every other one. The aircraft has several radios — VHF, HF and UHF — so we have the capability to communicate ashore as well as at sea and we possess a remarkably accurate navigation system that would aid in a search and rescue attempt. The INS in the Prowler is the same as that found in the F/A-18. You can do a three hour hop, travel 1000 miles and that system won't be more than a mile off when you return back to your base. We also have Ground Radar Mapping that assists in navigating.

'TAC Notes cover the prosecution of enemy ships at sea and War-at-Sea scenarios are designed for that purpose. We have some standard doctrine but it would depend on what the target is — a single ship or a battle group and how is it defended. Does it employ surface-to-air missiles and anti-aircraft guns, and are there land bases to help defend it. The War-at-Sea will also vary according to the number and complexion of the surface units.'

EA-6B Prowler Electronic Countermeasures Officer of VAQ-209 'Star Warriors'

'As soon as we come out with a new piece of equipment the Soviets come out with something new so it's a continuous battle, much to the delight of the defence industry. Given the sophistication and miniaturization of computer systems we could probably go back to the pilot and the ECMO, the two-man team that started 20 years ago with the EA-6A. The Soviets never throw anything away so all those old SAM-2s and -3s are still out there, plus their new stuff. The Soviets have been responding to our sophisticated ECM by building ECCM features to combat our ECMs. They feel that the EA-6B is a threat to their weapons systems, as we proved most notably in Libya and the Persian Gulf, so the "B" gave Soviet designers a lot of headaches trying to counter our jamming. Because their ECM isn't as sophisticated as ours they employ a lot more aircraft than we do. Their *Badger* is a basic noise jammer and they use chaff, a cheap and reliable way to jam. You don't need a sophisticated aircraft to lay chaff so that's what the Soviets do. There are, however, ways to beat chaff by using Moving Target Indicators and radars and when the chaff stops moving you can break out the aircraft targets. But more primitive radar systems are still susceptible to chaff attacks. If the radar operator has never seen it before and he gets a big white cloud on his screen it's going to take him awhile to figure out what's going on."

EA-6B Prowler Electronic Countermeasures Officer of VAQ-309 'Axemen'

'The first part of any mission is the brief. In it the four crew members will discuss how the mission will operate. The brief will include the aircraft's start-up procedures, taxying, "min-go" speeds, rotation and take-off speeds, and if we lose an engine at rotation what kind of climb rate will we have if we are land-launching or going off the ship. Decisions are made prior to setting foot in the aircraft on how specific emergencies are to be handled; what criteria constitute a take-off abort and what circumstances will call for an airborne ejection, and whether we will blow the canopy or go through it. We don't want to be caught in an in-between situation. Headings, nav way-points, radios and communications procedures are reviewed. On the ECM portion of the brief targets are discussed, what radar sites will be jammed, where these will be and at what time the jammers will come on, what type of modulations will be used and when will they be turned off. If we are carrying HARM we will also want to know under what conditions it will be used. While we are in the passive surveillance of enemy electromagnetic emmissions we will determine what and when information will be passed to the strike group regarding the enemy radar sites that are "up", and any discoveries of in-coming airborne threats to the fleet like hostile missiles that have been fired from a SAG (Soviet Battle Group comprised of four or five ships). Enemy aircraft or ground station emmissions might be reported as well.

'During the War-at-Sea one of the primary objectives is the suppression of ship-board radars and radar controlled weapons. It will depend on the make-up of the SAG as to what radars you will jam, what those priorities will be, how close we will get and what our position will be relative to the other strike aircraft. One tactic is to deceive them into thinking that they are looking at a whole strike group. Another is that under fear of attack by anti-radiation missiles they will turn off their search radars altogether. If we can create enough confusion to get our aircraft in to do their work then we've won the round.

The Prowler's active jamming system is carried in external pods, two beneath each wing. This tactical jamming system covers all of the anticipated hostile emitter frequency bands. Each of the tracking jammer pods contains two transmitters with steerable antennas and a track receiver, or exciter, that controls the transmitter. A ram-air turbine in the nose of each pod generates the electrical power for the units. The pods' transmitters provide coverage for seven selected frequency radar wavebands. Surveillance receivers are in the tail of the aircraft in a fairing. They also carry chaff and flare dispensers

'A brief aboard the carrier usually takes two hours. If it's an air wing evolution the strike lead will conduct the brief. Generally, one member of the crew will attend and he will then return and brief the rest of us on how the

Left The EA-6B Prowler was built from the ground up as an electronic countermeasures platform, unlike its predecessor the EA-6A. Pulling up for a drink is one of VAQ-309's aircraft; whilst the pilot concentrates on maintaining the probe-drogue link, the ECMO alongside him takes a few snaps of a formating F-14. In the air, the Prowler handles differently than the Intruder; it is heavier and not as forgiving; it is faster and the approach speed is higher. The Prowler has not experienced the wing fatique problems of the A-6, this being due mainly to its mission profile and relatively light stores carriage

operation will be conducted. After the brief we man-up. We will cut through Maintenance Control and check out the Aircraft Discrepancy Book to see how the "bird's" been holding up.

'The Pre-flight of the aircraft will vary. It depends on your crew position. If you're the pilot, then you and ECMO One – the guy in the right front seat next to you – will carry out the same inspection. Usually, we will both cover the aircraft completely, that way there are two sets of eyes covering all the items. One of the key items to check is that the pod's RAT (Ram Air Turbine) blades turn and that the correct transmitters have been installed. When that has been completed we can go ahead and get strapped in. All the cockpit switches at this point are "off" except for two; the air-conditioning and the generator. I'll follow the pilot through the Pre-start and Engine Start Checklists. Any indications from the Plane Captain that we have a tail pipe fire would initiate an immediate shut down. With both engines running it's time to check the Tactical Computer, radar, the CDI (Course/Deviation Indicator) and start the alignment procedures in the INS. While the pilot's running his checks in the left seat I will put in the nav-turn points and then we are ready to go.

'As part of their pre-flight planning and preparation the backseat ECMOs have their programmes that were developed on the TEAMS (Tactical EA-6B Mission Support) Machine to load into their tactical computers. Their computers will now have a specific mission loaded in for this assignment. With the Martin-Baker ejection seat armed we're ready to fly. Take-off requires an affirmative response from all the crew prior to launch. I'll be watching the gauges, fuel flow and for any annunciator lights that might decide to blink on, and the airspeed indicator as we transition to flight.

'After our take-off from the boat we will check in with strike on the assigned frequency and rendezvous. We will have strike TAC vectoring from the E-2 to an inbound point off to a SAG if it is a War-at-Sea. We will fly our briefed profiles and will use our own initiatives depending on the threat. As soon as we go through 5000 ft the guys in the back turn on the system and get ready to go. The pods will be on and will be getting "timed-out". They will get bogus assignments to see if they are operating properly; putting out the proper wattage and gauging the jamming power so that we know what kind of system degradation we will have before we get to the target. If equipment isn't working it might require a spare aircraft to be launched if the mission's success is that critical.

'In the backseat most of the planning is done with the TEAMS Machine before launch. If that hasn't been done it's hard to go to a back-up mode. A lot of planning is put onto what is basically a very expensive cassette tape which is plugged into the aircraft. Various displays can be called up on the computer screen – graphic representations of a piece of land, information on radar signals and their location and frequency.

'In the simplest scenario this is how the system would be employed. Because you know what you're looking for you will tell the system to look for specific

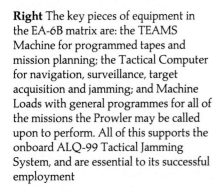

Right The key pieces of equipment in the EA-6B matrix are: the TEAMS Machine for programmed tapes and mission planning; the Tactical Computer for navigation, surveillance, target acquisition and jamming; and Machine Loads with general programmes for all of the missions the Prowler may be called upon to perform. All of this supports the onboard ALQ-99 Tactical Jamming System, and are essential to its successful employment

radar emissions. The system already knows what the electromagnetic parameters for that signal are, and when it finds the signal you've requested within those guidelines a symbol for that threat radar will appear on your screen. The direction to the signal will also be displayed. You will set your jammers up on that symbol, turn the "Master Radiate Switch" on and begin jamming. Usually though you're looking for more than one radar because you're jamming with a number of pods at different frequencies at different modulations and it can get complex in a hurry – all the more reason to do your homework before you get into the aircraft and get what you want on tape. There is no manual back-up mode in this aircraft. If you're not prepared you're out of luck.

'Sometimes we will accompany the bombers, sometimes we will have fighter cover. Back in 1983 when they were running a few TARPS F-14s over Beirut, they ran a Prowler off the coast to suppress missile radars along his track, and they had a fighter escort. If we were supporting the battle group or trying to suppress enemy bombers attacking we would have a fighter escort at that point also. If someone is shooting at us we don't have any way to shoot back so we

Above An 'Electric Intruder' of VAQ-309 'Axemen' from NAS Whidbey Island lands on the *Ranger*. An early ECM/Elint aircraft, the EA-6A was quickly developed during the Vietnam War in an attempt to try and stem the enemy's surface-to-air threat. Built as an interim measure before a formal ECM platform could be developed, the EA-6A had the same crude vacuum-tube technology as the EA-1 Skyraider and the EA-3 Skywarrior, the system carried being of immediate post-World War 2 vintage. Because the aircraft was 'cobbled' together, the reserves had no tactical, training or maintenance manuals for the EA-6A, patience and a sense of humour being much the order of the day for the VAQ units.

need some kind of protection. Standard doctrine for this kind of warfare says "the closer we are the lower we are, the further away we are the higher we will be". This rule is based on the depression angle of the jammers and the fact that they work better when they are used in this way.

'One of our least publicised roles is as a decoy. In the War-at-Sea scenario where we are going against the enemy's ships we will be high up in decoy mode. We will say, "here we are". We will throw out chaff and flares, plus commence jamming and basically do everything to get and keep their attention. We want their radars on us and their attention turned away from the other members in the strike group who are coming in from different angles.

'General tactics calls for us to take the enemy's air search early warning radar out first. If you force them to try and find you with their target tracking radars it's like trying to put a flash light beam on a pin in the sky. It's not easy to do because you don't know where to look to begin with. The target trackers then become our second priority. Some of the surface-to-air threats have been around a long time and are weapons we saw in Vietnam; the SA-2, -3, -4 and 6s. The "sixes" are the biggies. They are "home-on-jam" missiles. They're very capable and they give a lot of trouble. Depending on the missile we are capable of jamming it. If it's a command-guide weapon there are certain things that we can do to degrade the guidance. Laser and heat seeking missiles aren't within out capabilities. You're out of the spectrum with those.

'If our mission has us in escort mode we will probably, as part of the tactics that have evolved, break off early from the target and hit the egress radial as the bombers go in while we keep our jammers on the site. We will do a really flat turn because if we get our wing up the jammer's angle will be off so we try and do a quick, flat turn — sort of a skid — to the egress radial, jammers to the rear and we are out of there! If we are in stand off mode just outside the missile's range, we will just do flat turns in order to keep the jammers on the site at all times. Once we are back aboard the ship we will go to CVIC (Command Information Center) for a debrief. We will keep a written record of radars, radar sites and their locations and their frequencies in case we have to go back to the same site.

'The question of the jamming range versus the threat has often come up. This is a power battle. How much power can they put out versus how much can we put out. The closer we get the more our power is effective on their radar site. The further away we are the less effective it is. So the optimum is for us to be at an altitude and position that is just outside his missile's envelope, yet close enough that we can create the maximum jamming of their equipment. That's usually the game.

'Another facet of this cat and mouse game is the air defence of the battle group. One of our main jobs is to jam airborne targeting radar so that it forces the missile launch platform to get closer to where they think the target is. By doing that they will be getting closer to our F-14s who will take them out. The

Soviet *Bear*-Delta would probably be the most likely platform that we would encounter in that role. I would much rather have them shoot down the platform than have to contend with a missile.

'Getting back to the mission of the aircraft, we use ECM for "soft kills" to degrade, deceive and confuse the enemy's radar operators so that they cannot pick out the strike group or determine its position until the last possible moment. We will keep the strike group out of harm's way as long as possible to enable them to carry out their mission. When we no longer have the capability to degrade or deceive a radar system electronically then we will use HARM to "hard kill" the site. Either they keep it up or they turn it off. In any case they are degraded and either way we've done our job.'

Left Two EA-6As are hook down and in the pattern for landing aboard the carrier. Prominent on these aircraft are the ALQ-41/ALQ-100 forward emitting aerials, seen here as extensions of the underwing pylons, which are part of the deception jamming system. The large fin-tip fairing carries receiver aerials for the ECM system.

E-2C Hawkeye

E-2C Hawkeye Combat Information Center Officer of VAW-78 'Fighting Escargots'

'The E-2 has one of the more interesting and involved missions off the carrier. Our primary role in AEW (Airborne Early Warning) is working with the F-14s and F/A18s in interceptions of hostile aircraft. We fly with a crew of five. The pilots maintain the mission profile and assists with communications. In the back of the aircraft are the CICO (Combat Information Center Officer) who is the mission commander, and two air controllers. The equipment at each of the three stations is identical; any position can run any mission. You don't have to be in a certain seat to do a certain job. However, each scope can be tailored to a specific mission and this provides us with terrific flexibility.

'We will launch from the carrier 15 minutes before the fighters. If there is an E-2 already airborne and on-station he will give us information on all the contacts he has before he leaves. This is done computer-to-computer via Data Link. As the fighters come out we will pick them up on voice control as well as on Data Link. Any contacts that he has will appear on my screen with the contact's position, course, speed, heading and altitude and any information that I have will be automatically transferred to his scope. We will then vector them out to a holding point until we have a contact that must be identified, and then direct them to the contact. The overall air picture is run by the Air Control Officer, who is the anti-air warfare co-ordinator aboard ship. He is referred to as "Alpha Whiskey" and is responsible for 360° of the "pie". Our crew might only have a sector to guard. Unlike the Russian method of air-control, where there is rigid discipline of the fighter forces by ground controllers, we've reversed that and allow decisions to be made at the earliest opportunity by the fighter pilots who are in pursuit. So if communications are lost our system of decentralized control would assure that no bogey would slip through undetected.

Left What is the Hawkeye like to fly? Even with its great safety record, it is considered by many to be the most difficult aircraft to bring aboard the carrier. Inflight, the E-2 has pronounced 'Dutch roll', and characteristic of most aircraft when there is a power change, a trim change is mandatory as well. The 'Hummer' has increased in weight over the years from 50,000 to 53,000 lbs, so on a hot day with high humidity and a full bag of fuel aboard, if the pilot loses an engine at the time of launch from the carrier he will never be able to climb away on the power of a single Allison T56 alone. The manufacturer is planning an engine upgrade which will boost the power to 5100 hp per unit, greatly increasing the Hawkeye's single powerplant performance in the process

Above An E-2 of VAW-78 takes a trap aboard the *Eisenhower*. A day carrier qualification is good for one year and a night qual lapses after seven days. Once in the air, the E-2 is comfortable to ride in, and the cockpit layout is tailored especially for the pilots' needs. At cruise, the 'Fuel Condition Levers' are set at 1507 rpm, the engines' computers monitoring their performance

Left A 'Fighting Escargot' of VAW-78 sails past parked F-14s on the deck of the 'IKE'. During the reserve squadrons' cruise, both the maintenance personnel and technical representatives from aircraft manufacturers are on board to insure the safety and airworthiness of the machines. Launches and recoveries on the carriers put a big shock on the airframes so constant inspections are necessary

'In addition to our "active" radar we have a "passive" method of looking at an enemy's radar system. Once we get the emmissions "signature" from their radar we have a list of foreign aircraft that it could be associated with, and with that ID we can make certain assumptions on what weapons it might be carrying and take the appropriate action. However, the best way of identifying an aircraft is visually.

'Circumstances will determine how we will pursue the air war scenario and how the Rules of Engagement will be applied. Generally, we will not shoot until the hostile aircraft, once visually identified, shows hostile activity. This applies to a "cold war" situation. In a "hot war" anything that approaches the carrier, unless it can be identified as friendly based on an IFF interrogation, will be shot. You will not let him close to within 70 miles of the carrier! At any one time the air control officers may be handling five or more intercepts, each with new bogeys coming on-screen that have to be processed. It can become very hectic. New targets automatically receive a computer-generated symbol. There are different symbols that have been created for friendly and hostile surface and air targets. Fresh "track numbers" will also be assigned.

'To access target information we will place the tip of a "light pen" over the blip on our radar screen. This will "hook" the target and will "ask" the computer to provide course, heading, speed and altitude data on that contact. That information will be printed out on the bottom part of the scope. The computer interfaces with the radar, navigation and IFF systems and there is a 1500-page instruction manual that will allow you to use the system to its maximum limit. NFO training is 28 to 33 weeks to learn how to use the equipment and pilots will spend three to five months at the Fleet Replacement Squadron learning how to fly the E-2.'

E-2C Hawkeye Pilot of VAW-78 'Fighting Escargots'

'The E-2 is one of the most unstable aeroplanes to fly. At $55 million per copy every time there is a power change there's a change in trim. The ailerons are too small and the rudders aren't large enough to do the job. That huge dish on top of the aircraft actually makes it more stable. At 95° and 90 per cent humidity with a maximum fuel load and with 10° of flap – normal for a cat shot – if you lose an engine on the catapult stroke, which isn't uncommon, at that weight you would not have single-engine climb capability. You won't make it out of there. The E-2 has gone from 50,000 lbs to 53,000 lbs and that has really

Right Over the ramp, an E-2C of VAW-88 'Cotton Pickers' comes aboard the *Independence* (CV-62) during CVWR-30's sea tour. Reserve personnel are constantly augmenting active duty squadron, assuming flight crew positions with units in the Med, and elsewhere

Above With the catapult's blast barrier raised, the E-2 prepares to take the launch. Once airborne, things get pretty hectic, targets that appear on the aircraft's air and surface search radars automatically receiving 'track numbers'. These are computer-generated symbols created for friendly and hostile aircraft and ships, the computer interfacing with the on board radar, navigation and IFF interrogation systems to make this possible. Enemy aircraft can also be identified through their radar emmission signatures

Right As the catapult fires condensation forming at the prop tips of the E-2 causes ribbons of vapour to form. The AWACs leave the ship 15 minutes before the fighter aircraft in the wing. If there is an E-2 already on station, information regarding that crew's contacts will be passed from one aircraft's on board computer to that of its relief, via Data Link. Similarly, as the fighters transit to the CAP position the course, speed, heading and altitude of hostile contacts are passed to their scopes, the Tomcats being vectored to a holding point, or an intercept

The 'eye in the sky', the Grumman E-2C Hawkeye is the carrier-based, all-weather airborne command, control, communications and intelligence platform; C^3I for short. The Hawkeye's radar is capable of monitoring three million cubic miles of airspace. It expands the battle groups defence perimeter and enables it to detect approaching aircraft and surface threats. The five-man crew (two pilots and three NFOs) provides the air wing with strike and intercept control of their assets. Other missions that the reserve crews are called upon to perform include maritime surface surveillance, SAR co-ordination and automatic communications relay services. This Charlie model is with CVWR-30 and is from VAW-88 based at NAS Miramar

dragged the performance down. There is a need to increase the horse-power. We use one-third flap so that we have a higher end-speed and more knots behind us. But that puts a bigger shock on the airframe going off the boat 10 or 15 knots faster. We're now at 4600 horsepower and we're hoping for an engine upgrade in the future that will take it to 5100 horses. The redesigned engine will be more efficient and it will also give us greater loiter time. The "Hummer" is the hardest aircraft to land aboard the ship due to the poor directional control from the props. Every power change requires a corresponding change in the rudders and the elevator. It's a fistful landing on the ship. Once you take the cat shot it's easy. The hard part is the trap – getting it back on board.

'A day carrier qual is good for a year. The night qual lapses after seven days. Once we are in the air the aircraft doesn't require much work. There is an auto-pilot that holds the angle of bank and the altitude and centres the ball. This is a turboprop aircraft, a jet engine driving a propeller. Once we are at cruising altitude we will set the throttles – the "Fuel Condition Levers" – at 1507 rpm and then leave them alone. All changes are on demand and are controlled by a computer on each engine. There is no "mixture, prop pitch or carb heat" to worry about. The bail-out drill is easy. The main door is jettisoned and with arms folded, gripping the "D" ring with your right hand, you roll out the door. Gravity and the slip stream will pull you clear of obstructions – the engine nacelle, gear door and vertical stab. Despite its faults the aircraft is very comfortable to ride in. In the cockpit everything readily falls-to-hand and it shouldn't be forgotten that the aircraft has an excellent safety record. Our maintenance people and the manufacturer's technical representatives at the station and aboard ship are there to ensure the air worthiness of each aircraft.

'How does the E-2 avoid becoming a target? Usually, we will stand well off the coast, far enough away to make an interception by hostile forces unlikely. And we will have two Tomcats along for insurance!'

Right The failing light of day will not hamper this E-2's primary sensors; radar, IFF and passive detection. The Hawkeye's primary role is working with the F-14s and F/A 18s to achieve interceptions. The CICO (Combat Information Officer) and mission commander, plus two other air control radar operators can direct the 'friendlies' down to a mile separation from their target for a visual contact

Above Of all the aircrew who make up a carrier air wing, the guys with the most flying hours under their belts are invariably the E-2 Hawkeye jocks. Long incumbered with old and tired Alpha and Bravo model E-2s, the reserve Hawkeye units now fly the latest Charlie models, although the radar in these aircraft is slightly older than in the fleet's Hawkeyes. This silhouetted E-2C belongs to VAW-88 'Cotton Pickers'

Right Early morning and a naval reserve E-2 Hawkeye calls the tower for taxy clearance prior to departure. Since the Falklands War, airborne early warning has been a key topic on the international military agenda. The Brazillian Air Force and Navy actively sought E-2 participation in their *UNITAS XXVII* manoeuvres to help them evaluate the tactical advantages of AEW assets. Reserve squadron VAW-78 'Fighting Escargots' of CVWR-20 provided aircraft and crews for surface unit targeting and anti-surface warfare control for the exercise

P-3C Orion

P-3C Orion Tactical Co-ordinator of VP-69 'Totems'

'We usually begin with a brief at the ASWOC (Anti-Submarine Warfare Center). Its role is to evaluate intelligence data on air, surface and sub-surface activities and co-ordinate and direct the appropriate response. The brief will take anywhere from 30 minutes to one hour and will cover all the mission requirements. Because of the sometimes urgent nature of the missions there is always a maintenance group standing by ready to repair anything that requires last minute attention before take-off. Some of the flights are monitored up the chain of command by the Joint Chiefs so we want to be sure that we get off on time.

'Once airborne I'll send ASWOC a status report on the aircraft and the tactical crew will study the mission's parameters during the transit to our station. Often we will be relieving another aircraft or working with the battle group, and its aircraft and surface units, so check-in procedures will vary and will depend on who is already there. If there is a battle group it will have a senior officer who is in operational command and who will direct us. Through Data Link, encoded voice net, satellites, seabed hydrophones, teletype and our own acoustic gear, we are able to keep ASWOC, the battle group and the local tactical aircraft – LAMPS and Vikings – in the "loop". If we are working alone we might prosecute a target with tactics that are based solely on our own design or we might be directed by the ASWOC ashore.

'The Russian *Delta* and *Typhoon* class submarines have missiles with a range of over 4000 miles and are capable of targeting all of the US and Europe. A typical mission against a Soviet submarine would be to deploy a search pattern of sonobuoys. The two acoustic operators would be monitoring these while a non-acoustic operator would be monitoring radar or ESM (Electronic Surveillance Measures) to pick up the target on the surface. If they are down low he would be using the MAD (Magnetic Anomaly Detector) system to pick up any distortion in the Earth's magnetic field caused by the sub. Typically though we will be using the acoustic sonobuoys as our primary detector. Once

Right Seen here on maritime patrol, the P-3's mission is not confined to anti-submarine warfare. The Orion is equipped to carry conventional and nuclear weapons either internally or on underwing hardpoints. Torpedoes, mines, depth bombs and the AGM-84A Harpoon missile can also be employed for over-the-horizon targeting of enemy surface vessels

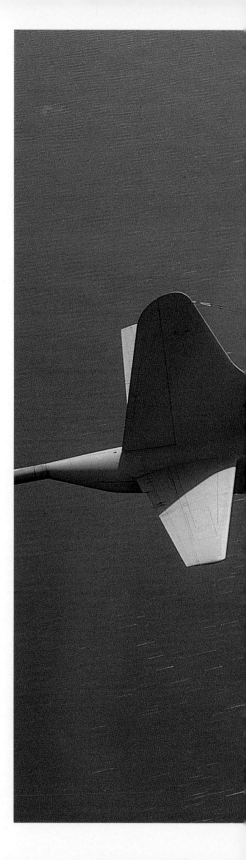

Left A reserve P-3 Orion with two A-7 Corsair IIs in-tow. There are 13 reserve patrol squadrons who are currently using the P-3A/B TACNAVMOD and P-3C UPDATE III aircraft

Below An Orion of VP-93 'Executioners'. Besides the national insignia and the word 'NAVY', reserve patrol aircraft carry no markings. Of the crew of 12, the Tactical Co-ordinator (the TACCO) is the man responsible for the mission's parameters being defined and for the plans execution. He will monitor, review and revise as the situation dictates, and he will make the ultimate decisions regarding 'search and kill' procedures, weapons selections and release

contact is gained we will prosecute with Directional Buoys and get down to attack criteria. Passive and active buoys are part of our equipment vocabulary as well and are used to "localize" the target.

'All the information from the operators' computers is fed to the TACCO's display so that I have a tactical summary of what is going on and can plan the next step in the attack. The pattern, spacing and orientation of the buoys we deploy can be varied depending on what tactics we are using. The information that the buoys send back is displayed as a series of dark marks, printed on a graph. These are called "Grams" and a submarine or surface ship will produce a certain frequency of mark. The acoustic operators are provided with publications that allow them to classify and identify targets based on these marks, or signatures.

'The submarine can try and use the state of the sea to hide. They have data on where the sea water temperature changes are, and the degree of those

changes. We drop buoys that will give us the sea's temperature profile; the characteristics of the water that we are over, allowing us to play that game as well.

'If we fire at a target that is submerged, sonobuoys will allow us to monitor the torpedo's run and we will of course hear the explosion. When the weapon is dropped from the aircraft there are altitude and speed restrictions that have to be met so they aren't destroyed. The torpedoes are programmed prior to loading but can be changed while enroute. The torpedoes have internal memories and some can have their track altered while they are running.'

Above The Navy's mission is control of the sea. It was for this purpose that the multi-mission, land-based P-3C Orion was designed. First and foremost, the Orion's primary role is to detect, track and destroy enemy submarines. The P-3's speed, all-weather day or night response and its legendary endurance on-station for periods of up to 14 hours make it well suited for the task. This VP-69 'Totems' P-3 has two engines feathered to extend its time on station over the Pacific. The Orion carries a full range of detection sensors including active and passive sonobuoys, DIFAR acoustic processor, MAD gear, radar, IRDS, ESM and cameras. An on board digital computer processes the mountain of avionics and nav data, supports the tactical displays of the ASW sensors and tactical plots, and monitors and launches ordnance

Left The Orion front office is big and roomy. Seven-tenths of the earth's surface is covered in water, and most P-3 crews will say that they've seen every inch. Not all missions performed by the P-3 are offensive in nature. The crew of one of VP-65's Orions was instrumental in the search and rescue of passengers aboard a downed missionary aircraft in the South Pacific in 1980. However, ASW work is essentially what pays the bills

SH-3H Sea King and HH-60H Seahawk

HH-60H Seahawk Pilot of HCS-5 'Firebirds'

'We used to fly the HH-1K "Huey Gunship" over in Vietnam during the war. As HAL-3 we were first headquartered at Vung Tau and then at Binh Thuy. In the five years we were in operation we ran up 35,000 hours "in country" and flight crews flew an average of 600 combat missions during a 12-month tour. We were more heavily armed in the "Huey" than we are in the new HH-60. We had a GAU-2B/A Gatling type mini-gun with 4000 rounds, two door-mounted M-60s and two rocket launchers with seven 2.75 in FFARs (Folding Fin Aerial Rockets). The Dash-60 has only two M-60Ds, but a lot of our work is at night and we don't plan on having many gunfights. The reserve HCS Squadrons have 10 years and 8000 hours of goggle time. No-one comes close to that. Night insertion and extractions of BUDS and SEAL Teams are part of the Special Warfare doctrine. At the Naval Strike Warfare Center we will work with the reserve air wings and a complete strike rescue package is put together; fixed wing TACAIR assets, helicopters and SEAL squads. This allows us to practise high and low threat strike rescues of downed aircrews during day and night evolutions and gives the SEALs an opportunity for fastroping, spierigs, and paradrops onto the high desert. It also gives the aircrews the chance to see how their aircraft operate at a high density altitude. As somebody said: "Fallon is where the rubber meets the road, where we get a chance to fly the terrain, to really hone our mission skills and to see what heppens".

'Some of the other duties we can be tasked with include Forward Air Control, naval gunfire spotting, overhead convoy escort and as a night aerial reconnaissance platform. Like the old HAL-4 and -5, our key personnel are trained by MAWTS-1 (Marine Aviation Weapons and Tactics Squadron-One) as Weapons and Tactics Instructors.'

Right An SH-3H Sea King helicopter of HS-75 'Emerald Knights' hovers before departing on an arduous, bone-jarring ASW mission. As part of their training syllabus the unit will deploy to fleet aircraft carriers, small and major combatants and auxiliaries, as well as to ships of the Canadian Navy. The unit's secondary mission is SAR (search and rescue); the recovery of downed aircrews. Long-range AQS-13 sonar and AQS-80 towed MAD equipment developed specifically for helicopters, are used to prosecute enemy submarine targets

Left A SH-3H Sea King of HS-75 transitions from level flight into ground hover above the deck of the USS *Eisenhower* (CVN-69), having just returned from plane guard duty. The 'Emerald Knights' provide support for CVWR-20's carrier qualification and cyclic ops evolutions whilst carrying out their own independent ASW training. The squadron was established at NAEC Lakehurst, New Jersey, in 1970 as one of four 'citizen patriot' HS units. During a reserve reorganization the squadron moved to Willow Grove, Pennsylvania, in 1979, and then to balmier climes in 1985 with their current move to Jacksonville

Above Presently there are no permanent fixed wing anti-submarine aircraft assigned to the reserves. This coverage is provided by five helicopter squadrons; HSLs-74, -84, -94 and HS-75 and -85. These units are the ASW arm of CVWR-20 and CVWR-30, their operational control resting with Commander Helicopter Wing Reserve at NAS North Island. Other units under his charge are Helicopter Mine Countermeasures (HM) squadrons -18 and -19, and Helicopter Combat Support (HCS) squadrons -4 and -5. Hovering over the waters off Point Mugu, dipping its acoustic gear, is a Sea King of HS-85 'Golden Gators'

Left A plan view of two of HS-75's SH-3H Sea King helicopters, their main rotors folded, next to the 'island' on the deck of the *Eisenhower* during CVWR-20's ACDUTRA. The SH-3 on the left in glossy white paint still carries the squadron's colourful green markings on the rotodome cover, wheel sponson tips and within the waist band. A decal of the squadron's logo is on the spray guard in front of the engine intakes. The Sea King on the right is wearing the dour low-viz grey scheme typical of the aircraft of the fleet in the 1990s. The deck crews' jerseys are colour-coded to their tasks; red shirts handle ordnance; greens secure the aircraft to the catapults; whites are aircraft inspectors; and yellows are aircraft taxy directors who are responsible for the safe transit of the machines from one point on the deck to another. These men are ship's company and are not part of the personnel of the embarked air wing

Above The HH-60Hs of HCS-4 and -5, and their mission of combat support, are a straight line derivative of the Navy's Cobra gunship support that was provided the 'Brown Water Navy' in the Mekong Delta during the Vietnam War. Quick reaction time and close air support to the BUDs, SEALs, Special Warfare Groups and other Riverine Forces were, and still are, the hallmark of these squadrons. Tasked with the armed recovery of downed aircrewmen, and the day and night insertions and extraction of special groups behind enemy lines, these units can operate from fixed bases or surface vessels

Left The newest aircraft type to enter service with the reserve is the formidable Sikorsky HH-60H Seahawk, this helicopter being tasked with the roles of combat support and combat rescue (SAR) of downed aircrew. Assigned to HCS-5 'Firehawks', the helicopter is exclusively operated by the reserve. To help it complete its dangerous task, the HH-60H is fitted with an APR-39 radar warning receiver, ALE-39 chaff dispenser, ALQ-144 infrared jammer, night vision compatible lighting, infrared suppressors and an M-60 machine gun. Besides HCS-5, which fly out of NAS Point Mugu, California, sister squadron HCS-4 provides combat SAR for CVWR-20 from its base at NAS Norfolk, Virginia

C-9B Skytrain II

C-9B Skytrain II Pilot of VR-61 'Islanders'

'One day the President, through the Joint Chiefs of Staff, decides that it would be a prudent idea to make our presence known somewhere in the world. A ship is selected for the "power projection", and so is a date for deployment. When a ship's movement is scheduled, message traffic goes down to ensure that not only is the vessel ready, but also that the people who man it and the supplies are there as well. That's where we get involved. The message comes to us and it says that the ship is going to leave on Monday the 22nd so we need all the supplies and people there on the 21st. From there, our scheduling command tasks specific aeroplanes to carry the goods.

'We operate seven days a week here and have a full-time staff of TAR personnel who do the flying. When we receive the tasking message we will start making the calls for the aircraft commanders, most of whom will be selected reservists.

'We fly with an aircraft commander, co-pilot and crew chief in the cockpit. We also carry a load master and flight attendants. Two hours before the flight everyone shows up to work on the mission and the flight schedule is printed. The co-pilot will fire-up the computer and get a flight plan for the route we will be taking. This programme gives fuel, time, distances, way-points, navaids, recommended altitudes, fuel minimums, winds aloft, drift, time-on-route, fuel remaining, mission number and the weather. This is all filed with CONUS ATC (Continental United States Air Traffic Control) for an IFR flight. The computer that provides this information is located at the Naval Post Graduate School in Monterrey, California. At the same time the load master is checking to make sure that there aren't going to be any problems here, or down range, and he will

Right From the earliest times military commanders have acknowledged the need to have a reliable store of supplies and an even surer method for their delivery. The reserve's fleet logistic support squadrons provide round-the-clock worldwide movement of men and material for the Navy and Marine Corps, the reserve and the regular forces. The squadrons operate the McDonnell Douglas C-9A/B Nightingale and Skytrain II aircraft, which replaced the fleet's ageing and venerable C-118B Liftmasters in the late 1970s. The C-9B is the Navy's version of the commercial DC-9, and it can be configured either to carry 107 passengers or 27,000 lbs of cargo on 88 in by 108 in military freight pallets. It is also able to carry a mixed load of passengers in the rear and cargo forward, and is manned by a crew of six. The aircraft's high-lift devices and anti-skid systems make the take-offs and landings less worrisome events

often call-ahead to make sure that if it is a load we are going to be picking up it will be palletized properly, particularly if we are in "G-Rig" where the pallets are inserted sideways into the aeroplane instead of the long way. The crew chief meanwhile, is preparing the aircraft in the form of a pre-flight and is getting all the check lists taken care of. The co-pilot will get the cockpit set up with all the glowing switches "on" and all the dull ones "off", and will get the INS programmed. The crew chief and the aircraft commander will stop at Quality Assurance and Maintenance Control, who will assure us that all is ready for the flight. Thats includes oil and gas and that all the tool boxes and all the tools are accounted for. This prevents leaving screw drivers and pliers in strange and dangerous places. I'll read over any past discrepancies, sign the log and we will be ready to go.

'When I visually pre-flight the aeroplane I am looking for anything that's not normal. We don't want to see any leaks, any puddles of fluid on the ground, chunks of frozen ice and snow on the top surfaces, any dents or worn tyres. For the engine start the co-pilot will look outside to make sure that the "Fire Watch" is manned and stays on-station. Before we start the aeroplane's engines they will make sure there is no-one behind us. We don't want to blow anyone over.

'The engine start is pretty much fool proof. The engines are control metered through the fuel control system. Everything is computerized so when you bring the fuel and the RPM on it's all automatic until it gets to "Idle". This takes into account turbine temperatures and inlet pressures and all kinds of mirrors and springs. All of this costs a lot of money, lasts a long time and is a big payroll deduction if you screw it up. As soon as you start to move forward you will select slats extended, flaps fifteen. This sets the jet up for flight and precludes FOD damage by directing the airflow such that it stops trash being sucked up into the engine.

'While taxying we will maintain a look-out doctrine to ensure that we aren't crossing an active runway or taxying a wing tip into anything. We will steer the aircraft with the nose wheel steering and the engines. We will also use the brakes, but judiciously. Since you're 50 ft away from the wheels when you hit the brake it puts a tremendous twisting moment on that main wheel mount. With that brake locked that tyre has become like an erasure, it's scurrying around, screwing itself into the ground. Another thing, when making turns with a big aircraft you have to put yourself mentally back over the main gear since that's where the pivot point is. You have to be constantly aware of where the rest of the aeroplane is when you are on the ground.

'When we start to roll and we are still on the ground and something happens we can stop. After the call of V-1 it will be an airborne emergency and, with the exception of silencing the bell if it's an engine fire or confirming that the ignition switch is in over-ride, you don't do anything until you have passed through 800 ft! You don't want to start shutting down or doing anything tricky low to the ground because in the excitement you could find that you've shut

Wingtip lights twinkling, this C-9B has just lifted off from NAS Alameda, California, on its way across the Pacific. During this mission the reserve Skytrain II will perform the role of 'pathfinder' for a group of Marine Corps F-4s heading for Hawaii. Capable of providing reliable communications and precise navigation through its Omega and INS systems, the C-9B is ideally suited to this task. As a pathfinder, precise briefings are necessary with the flight leaders prior to the mission, as well as with the KC-130 tankers and the 'Duck-Butts' (the air/sea rescue aircraft). HF, UHF and VHF channels will all be used for communication between the aircraft and shore stations while enroute

down your only good engine and that it's the other one that's on fire. At that point you could run out of ideas, altitude and airspeed fast. So, in those situations, it's best to wind your watch; to just sit on your hands for a while. Passing 800 ft we will start to bring the flaps up and get into a cruising configuration at 250 knots with the gear up.

'About 120 miles out we start making preparations for the approach; we will review the most probable runway that will be assigned and the present conditions on the ground. Ranches, farms and factories all become distinct as we slide in over them to our landing. We will call Ground Control and give them a "heads-up" so that their fork-lifts, fuel trucks and personnel will be aware that we're coming in. Generally, we fly into military facilities but we also go into civilian fields. The C-9 is pretty good about landing. It is like most light aircraft. It's fairly honest in its flair, as far as its approach to landing, however the main mounts are behind the centre of pressure so you can rotate them into the ground when you pull back. If you have a good arrested rate of descent as you bring the nose up you can make a fairly smooth landing. With the aeroplane's weight on the tyres the spoilers will come up right away and destroy the lift.

'Generally, we will fly from 31,000 to 37,000 ft over the United States. We also have a mission where we fly over water with passengers and cargo or as a Pathfinder. Generally these flights require more planning as there are more contingencies to be considered. One of these is the "Equal Time Point", or the "Point of No Return", where you are half-way across and should something go

Above 'There is only one class in military air transport service and that is first class'
goes an old reserve addage. Indeed, boarding this sleek and spotless C-9 one would err
to expect less. The aircraft is manned by a pilot, co-pilot, loadmaster and two or three
flight attendants. Flights over the US are logged, as are all IFR journeys, with civil air
traffic control (ATC). On trans-oceanic hops the crew will file a flight plan with ATC
and with the Oceanic Control Agency as supervisor. Since there is no radar over the
oceans a mandatory reporting system has evolved where aircraft report in every 10°,
every hour. This keeps people from running into each other and in case of emergency
will automatically limit the rescuers' search area. Air routes overseas, reporting points
and radio frequencies for communications are on standard oceanic charts

wrong will you decide to continue on or turn back. As a Pathfinder we've been the communications base and the flight lead for a group of 10 F-4s and were charged with the responsibility of safely getting them across a large body of water. When you're involved in a Pathfinder mission it requires a lot of briefings with various flight leaders, as well as with the tankers and the "Duck Butts" – the rescue aircraft. The tanking tasks tended to be carried out by USMC KC-130s in the past, however, now much of that mission has been taken over by USAF KC-10s because they can provide tanking capability as well as rescue, and can also act as the communications platform.

'Typically we would take-off first and the F-4s would catch us and would fly on our wing. At 400 miles out we would rendezvous with a tanker and they would take on the fuel to get to Hawaii. Two-hundred miles out of Hawaii there would be another tanker heading our way and they would refuel again, which would allow them to make it all the way across. That takes a lot of co-ordination, a lot of chatter on the HF, UHF and the VHF radios. HF is used for jet to jet communication, and to talk to maintenance facilities and to get on-ground links to talk to your squadron's office back at the home base, or to your wife. UHF is a short range military frequency; military fighters are all on UHF. VHF is used for general radio communications with ATC civilian radio traffic.

'As part of the transport community we will carry anything that has to do with the military. We've transported Army Special Forces Teams, SEAL Teams, Rangers and members of the Delta Force. It doesn't matter what branch of the service they're in. If they are part of the military we carry "em!

'During over-water flights mandatory reports are required every hour, every 10°. Because there is no radar over the ocean a reporting system based on time estimates has evolved, with the Oceanic Control Agency as supervisor. If we were going to Europe we would file an IFR departure from the US giving our destination to the ATC. They aren't just going to say "take-off and give us a call when you get there". They want you at a certain point at a certain time. This keeps people from running into each other. If you're overdue it will limit the search area. As you hit each fix you will call in your altitude, fuel state and estimated time to the next fix. The trans-oceanic air routes, reporting points, stations and frequencies are on the Oceanic Charts. While you are calling in you will hear others at different waypoints – Charlie, Delta, Echo – people in front and behind you and at different altitudes who will also be calling in.

'The Navy's original procurement request to McDonnell Douglas was for a passenger aeroplane similar to their DC-9 configuration. The airlines wanted the MD-80 so McDonnell shut the DC-9 production line down. The Navy then went out into the used plane market and bought them at considerably less cost than if they had been purchased new. Besides people and their baggage, we carry spare parts for aircraft, typewriters for the administration people, personal effects and engines. These aircraft were originally designed to carry people but have since been modified to carry cargo and passengers. We will transport anything that the Navy needs.'

KA-3B Skywarrior and A-4F Skyhawk

Left This KA-3B Skywarrior of VAK-208 is seen aboard the USS *Ranger* (CV-61). The 'Jockeys', like their West Coast sister squadron VAK-308 'Griffins', had a broader range of responsibilities that embraced more than just tanking other aircraft; they were tasked with long-range over water pathfinding and low-level navigation for the tactical squadrons of the reserve and regular fleet. Originally, both squadrons carried the VAQ designation as Tactical Electronic Warfare units, and they only became VAK designated in 1979. The aircraft's high wing configuration, and the position of its landing gear relative to the mass of the airframe, has given rise to the descriptive term 'doing the Whale Dance' to describe the KA-3's movements during an arrested landing

Overleaf The view from the NFO's seat in an F-14 is as good as you can get during mid-air refuelling, tanking services in this instance being provided by a 'Whale' of VAK-308. The green-red-green lights on the tanker's belly are used by the receiver for the line-up prior to engaging the basket. Inflight refuelling is dangerous so a light touch on the controls and a laid back attitude are ingredients for a 'first pass into the basket'. At night in bad weather with 'bingo fuel', the 'Whales' were always a welcome sight

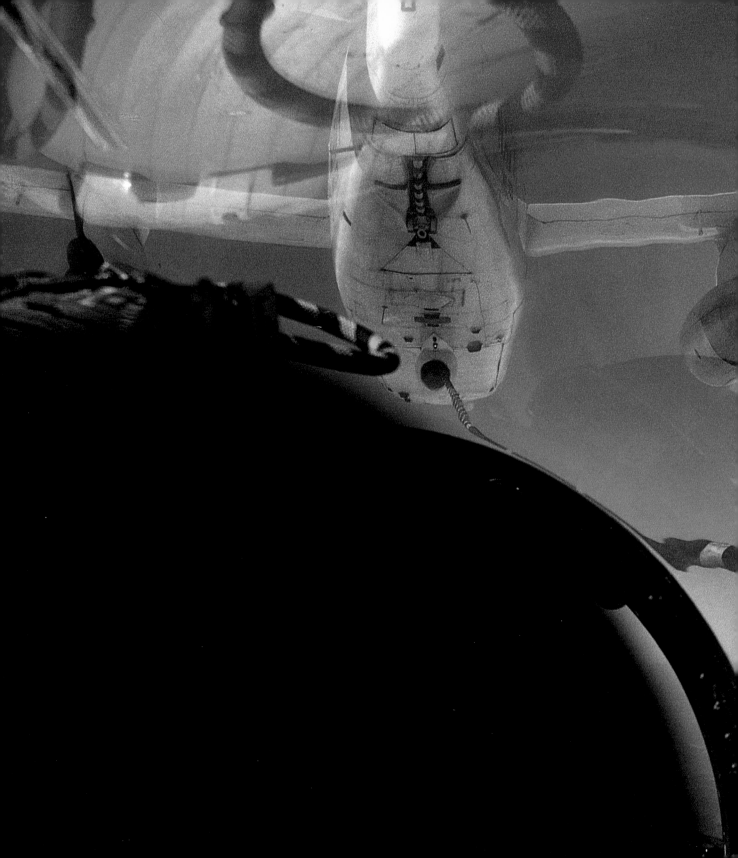

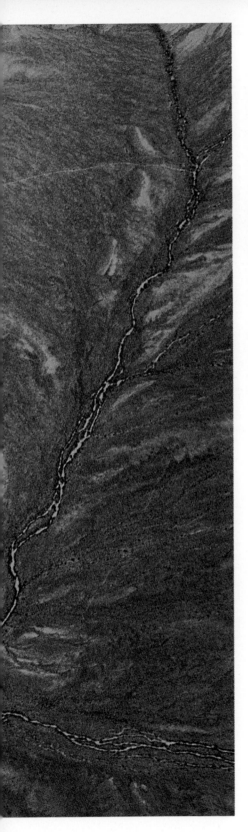

Left and above A KA-3 of VAK-308 with an F-14 of VF-302 'on the basket' are seen here cruising over Yuma. Once the standard frontline and reserve carrier-based aerial tanker, the KA-3 has been replaced by KA-6D Intruders throughout the fleet on both coasts. At the time of their retirement many of the KA-3s still carried some ELINT and ECM equipment, relics from an earlier life with the Navy

Above Three A-4Fs of VFC-13 carry the Red Star, emphasizing their role as 'bad guys', and making the aerial duels a bit more realistic. Each aircraft appears to carry a slightly different non-specular grey tactical paint scheme, the aircraft closest to the camera wearing a dark grey national insignia and intake warning bars whilst the other A-4s in the formation display a light grey variant of the same details. 'Saint Two-Zero' has also had some recent repair work performed on the port wing's upper surface where an apple-green zinc chromate patch of paint is evident. These aircraft are returning from running an intercept against CVWR-30's Alpha strike at NAS Fallon

Left Both reserve adversary squadrons use the A-4F Skyhawk aircraft, these particular jets hailing from VFC-13 'Saints', based at Miramar. Although a reserve unit, the 'Saints' provide adversary training for fleet fighter squadrons all year round. The 'Saints' trace their history back to 1946 when the unit was established on the F6F-5 Hellcat. Over the years the following types have appeared on the squadron books at one time or another; FG-1D/F4U-4 Corsair, F9F-2 Panther, AD-1NA Skyraider, F9F-8 Cougar, FJ-3/-4 Jury, A-4B/C/F/L/E Skyhawk, F-8H Crusader and the TA-4J. Originally based at New Orleans, the unit moved to NAS Miramar in 1976 as demand for DACT services and other fleet support missions increased. The unit's sister-squadron, VFC-12 'Omars' at NAS Oceana, Virginia, started life at NAS Sand Point, Seattle, Washington, in 1943, equipped with F4F Wildcats and TBM Avengers. The VFC's role in fleet training started in 1975 when they became part of the reserve. The 'Omars' operate 12 TA-4J and 2 A-4F aircraft and have a complement of 21 officers and 189 enlisted personnel. Perhaps the 'hottest' (but definitely the oldest) aircraft currently in service with the reserve, the A-4F 'Super Fox', is powered by a Pratt & Whitney J52-P-408 engine, which produices 11,200 lbs of thrust. This gives the A-4F a thrust-to-weight ratio of roughly one to one, enabling the diminutive Skyhawk to maintain forward momentum in the vertical (something that the A-model Tomcat struggles to achieve)

Above Re-engined and stripped of weapons except for TACTs wiring, these aggressor aircraft outperform all the Navy's fighters bar the similarly tasked F-16N. In the air, 50 per cent of the squadron's time is spent simulating the flight and fighting characteristics of Soviet and Red Chinese tactical aircraft. Learning the traits, tactics and capabilities of the MiG and Sukhoi series of aircraft from the 'Saints' and 'Omars' keeps the F-14 and F/A18 fighter jocks honest and on their toes

Right The two-seat TA-4Js and the A-4Fs of VFC-13 provide realistic hands-on-hardware air combat readiness practice for surface units like the AEGIS missile cruisers. The 'Saints' are also regular visitors to the Air Force Fighter Weapons School and the Navy's TOPGUN. Canadian Armed Forces and USMC units also make use of the 'bogey men'. The unit's 18 pilots average a total of 2000 flight hours per year, and the A-4 airframes are projected to be flying through to the year 2005. It takes two airmen 30 minutes to refuel, troubleshoot any 'gripes' and turn the aircraft around, ready for the next hop

Overleaf Flying on the edge of the envelope and swapping airspeed for altitude, this A-4F starts to go pure vertical as its opponent sails by underneath. The TACTS pod carried on its centreline records the aircraft's airspeed and attitude and transmits the data to the computer at the Display and Debrief Center back at base, where it will be recorded for replay. With this system both the attacker and the quarry have their moves taped for posterity – you will know who got shot down and why. Playing the role of a 'Red' defender going for the interception, this A-4 will be guided by GCI (ground controlled intercept) just as a Soviet aircraft would in real-life. Over Dixie Valley and the Bravo-17 Range at Fallon, the F-14s and F/A-18s of an attacking force will be bounced by the 'Saints' as they try to enter the 'enemy airspace'